THE BLIND LEADING THE BLONDE ON THE ROAD TO FREEDOM

Confessions of a Recovering Spiritual Junkie

Nurit Oren

Published by Gabor Harsanyi
Budapest, Hungary

Book cover and internal design by Jane Green of Everlasting Magic Design.
design@everlastingmagic.com
www.everlastingmagicdesign.com

Photography by Eva Harsanyi

ISBN – 978-963-12-3336-0

ACKNOWLEDGMENTS

The inspiration to write this book came from the people in Tatabanya, Hungary, who asked me to speak at their Monday Five O'clock High Tea gathering, sponsored by Katalin Boldog. Seeing the love on their responsive faces, and the transforming effect that my words had on them, made me realize the importance of revealing what you are about to read. So thank you lovely Tatabanyans, thank you Katalin Boldog and many thanks to my dear friend and Cosmic Troubadour, Iby Duba, who introduced Gabor and me to this wonderful group and to the magic embedded within the Hungarian language.

Additional inspiration came from many engaging and eye-opening conversations with my friend Barbara Whiting Young, Managing Director of Robert A. Young & Associates. Thank you Barbara from Santa Barbara for your love and support.

Many heartfelt thanks as well to Jerry Katz, for writing a wonderful foreword; Dr. Zoltán Szabó, Robert Rabbin and Sarolta Illés for sharing their impressions of the book; Gina Rabbin for her expert editing; and Jane Green for the interior and cover design of this book.

I also want to thank the many people who opened doors for me or simply "pushed" me along the way over the years, such as Spiritual Mentor and Relationship Coach, Sylvia Abergil, Israel Sushman of I. Sushman Constulting and "Coachgirl" Chandra Alexander, to mention just a few.

Much gratitude goes to my dear friend Robert Rabbin for his sincere, generous and honest feedback, coaching, guidance and, most importantly, for his fearless courage to ask a blonde, double Leo, former Israeli army girl to remove a few hundred excessive exclamation points from her book!!!!!!!!!! !!!!!!!!!!!!!!!!!!!! A friend like him is rare indeed.

DEDICATION

This book is dedicated to the love of my life, the angel who has lifted me out of a 40 year dead-end spiritual search, has shown me the way home, and who continues to guide me and walk with me on my road to silence. Without your constant love, care and wisdom, this book would never have come into existence. Csendmester Gabor, this is for you:

I searched and toiled from morning till night,
Dazzled by words and visions of light.
I was told I am THAT a long time ago,
"You'll know it in TIME," but there hides the foe!

After so many years the truth did show up.
The control of the mind I had to give up.
It's not in the east, nor in the west;
Neither past nor future offer true rest.

It's NOW or never that stillness exists;
Our very own birthright we seemed to have missed!
But once it is known, you're secure and sound,
Cause the magic of being is what you have found!

TABLE OF CONTENTS

CHAPTER THREE
SECOND MISDIRECT: IN RETROSPECT, IT WAS INTELLECT

CHAPTER FOUR
ALONE AT LAST, FOR BETTER OR FOR WORSE

CHAPTER FIVE
MY SPIRITUAL PATH CAN FINALLY START. BRING IT ON!

FOREWORD

The hunger to know "truth" may be the greatest grace of all, yet the search that ensues often looks graceless. Nurit was caught by more than one guru's self-indulgence, emphasis on spiritual concepts, and affectation.

It happens. It is as though one gets blindfolded by those who themselves are blindfolded, gets spun around, and then is given a scent of truth, while the source of the scent never drops into one's mouth. Much time, money, and freedom is given away in the chase of "external hoopla," as Nurit calls it. To me the hoopla is like the midway at the carnival.

Onto Nurit's pursuit fell a cool and torrential rain that swept away the cotton candy sellers and the games of chance. And the blindfolds. In Nurit's case that rainfall was known as Gabor Harsanyi, more simply called her teacher.

With the blindfolds gone, it was recognized that being leads being.

And then what? What happens after being recognizes being, or when this recognition is renewed, or when it becomes an unbroken presence?

Then it is possible to live intelligently and effectively, a life of some balance and ease. A sense of balance and ease, I believe, characterize the lives of Nurit and Gabor. I didn't mention they are now married.

Still, I don't imagine that stumbling and gracelessness completely come to an end. It's hard to undo all the spiritual concepts screwed into our perceptual filters. But we can keep becoming more and more aware of what we are doing and how we are behaving, while remembering to turn to inner silence.

This book demonstrates that the fundamental hunger to know truth will prevail. For most of us, as for Nurit, it is a journey from blindfolds to being.

Jerry Katz, founder, Nonduality Salon
www.nonduality.com

INTRODUCTION

> **Watch out for the nude guy who offers you the shirt off his back!**

Sharing my story by writing this book has actually been an excruciating experience for me, since it kept revealing to me how much hold my former teachers still had on me. It is not my intention to antagonize anyone, but rather to assist those who have reached the kind of confusion that mental spirituality breeds and fosters.

There are countless teachers and mentors out there who will guide us on an endless search to find what we already are, while their teachings remain on the level of the mind and the ego. But guess what? It is the very mind or ego that keeps what we are searching for hidden so well. Unfortunately, very few are calling their bluff. It is high time that it finally be announced: *The King Has No Clothes*. The red dot on the forehead, the orange robes and the flow of spontaneous mystical poetry just don't cut it anymore.

Why is it that so many find it easy to be out-spoken about corrupt governments, crooked politicians and corporations like Monsanto who poison our food – I see it on Facebook all the time and mostly agree with it – yet when it comes to blowing the whistle on a spiritual teacher who intellectually poisons so many spirits, most people either pretend they don't see it, or they make all kinds of self-defeating statements they picked up at some new-age seminar such as, "It's not right to judge" or "I attracted this" or "I created this and I have to own it" or "I choose to focus on the good that I got?"

Awakened teachers are not interested in enslaving their disciples and keeping them chained to their teachings. If they did, they would be giving up their own freedom.

> **If you have not turned inside, your spiritual path has not started yet!**

THE BLIND LEADING THE BLONDE ON THE ROAD TO FREEDOM

Confessions of a Recovering Spiritual Junkie

Nurit Oren

Chapter One

ONE FLEW OUT OF THE WORLD-VIEW NEST

Born To Be Wild

I was born in Kibbutz Sasa, situated in the north part of the Galilee in Israel. Much to the surprise of my mother, the midwife and the doctors, I burst out laughing as soon as I could take my first breath. I had golden blonde hair, chubby rosy cheeks, and looked like a bright yellow flower, so they named me Nurit, which is Hebrew for Buttercup.

My parents were atheist Jewish pioneers. They came from Canada to build this little settlement, and this is where I spent the first six years of my childhood. In those days children did not live with their parents, but rather in a children's home with a group of kids and an adult who looked after them. We only got to see our parents for a quick 4 p.m. visit and a good-night kiss before going to bed.

There was no family unit to relate to, no mom and pop setting rules and enforcing discipline, and no one indoctrinating me into their inherited or acquired beliefs, opinions and concepts. No one told me what to do and how to do it, nor did they restrict me in any way. All I had was pure freedom and tons of energy. When I sat on my father's shoulders during our brief visits, I thought everyone else was a statue in contrast to my blissful aliveness.

It was a very visceral experience. I was allowed to be wild, to play naked in the mud, to fight with the dogs around the garbage bins trying to find leftovers, to pull out and relish a fresh green pepper from the ground, to milk a cow or walk in her shit, to wander in the hills of the Galilee picking up rocks and smelling wild flowers. I rarely wore shoes. Those were the happiest days of my youth.

From Nature To Syphilization

At the age of six my unrestricted, unleashed and unbridled freedom was snatched away from me without a warning. The sturdy branch that held my blissful swing in life was brutally chopped off. My parents decided to leave the kibbutz and go back to Canada for a few years, so that my father could complete his education. All of a sudden I found myself in a strange country with a new language, and having to go to school for the first time.

The weather was so cold that running around naked or barefoot was out of the question. And the culture, totally different. This was an uptight conservative civilization that wouldn't know freedom if it bit its people on the ass. I soon discovered how cruel kids can be. I was not like them, and so they hit and teased me. There was one African American girl in my class.

I had never seen anyone like her before, and could not, for the life of me, understand why she was shunned. I thought she was so beautiful and looked like chocolate, so I became her best friend.

But the worst of all was that now, for the first time in my short yet entire life, I was living in a family unit with parents, a brother and grandparents. In came the dos and don'ts, the rules, the boundaries and expectations about everything, from no more running to speaking in a soft and polite tone. And now the reprimands, the high pitched scoldings, the punishments and the spankings were ushered in as if they were the only hope my parents had to ever succeed in taming the free spirited young girl they knew so little about.

Since we had no money, we had to live with my grandparents, religious Eastern-European Jews who forced us to go to synagogue every Saturday. This was certainly tough on my atheist parents who, for some reason, thought that secretly sneaking a Christmas tree into the basement would ease up the religious pressure. But needless to say, for someone like me who started out life with little to no values and concepts, this was quite confusing.

The shock of this whole move was so unbearable that I refused to speak for a year and a half, and after that I spoke only in English. I blocked out all memories of the wonderful kibbutz and forgot all my Hebrew.

After three years in Canada my family moved back to Israel, but not to the kibbutz. We now lived in a nice house in Bat-Yam, a suburb of Tel Aviv. School was a nightmare, as I had to re-learn Hebrew as if it was a new language. Once again I was the foreign kid trying to fit in. I was consistently searching for my lost freedom and my days of happiness were becoming a vague memory.

My best friend was a Yemeni girl, and at times I would secretly go with her to the Yemeni synagogue, where I enjoyed the rapturous singing and dancing. I had no regard for religion or God; I just wanted to be around happy people. Of course, I had to hide this from my parents, who believed that this kind of behaviour was an escape from life's harsh reality. And what if it was? What made them experts on "reality" anyway?

During my teen years, my only comfort was my father who, in spite of his opinions about reality, seemed to be a free spirit and an "outside the box" thinker. He became a famous detective with the Israeli police force after successfully identifying Adolf Eichmann, one of the major organizers of the holocaust in Germany.

Later on, my dad left the police force and became a well-known sculptor. He was now a bohemian artist with longish hair and a gigantic mustache. He wore rugged jeans way before they became "hip" in Israel, rode a golden motorcycle and scolded my teachers when they had the nerve to call him in just because I skipped a day of school. He introduced me to art, let me work with him in his studio and took me to every opera that came to town. For quite some time he was my best friend, which helped me get through the pain of losing my freedom.

If You Can't Beat Them, Join Them

As much as I looked forward to the end of high school, with its intimidating exams, hours of confinement and useless homework, the next event to take place in my life – joining the army – was not exactly the exciting breakthrough I was expecting. All my attempts to escape this civil duty had failed, and I was drafted for two years of service.

The first few months were intense and rigorous, as I was training from 5 a.m. to 10 p.m., when the lights went out. There was no time or energy left to think or complain, and harbouring any personal desire was completely hopeless. The only thing I could do, or had to do to survive, was to simply follow orders. To my mind this couldn't have been more "the opposite of freedom." However, to my great astonishment, I found myself rather content.

Could it be that not having my own way in just about everything temporarily stopped my mind from running its endless loop? Was I feeling relaxed since I was relieved of my decision-making function and the responsibility that came with it? I realize today that I was a lazy thinker since I did not know how to think.

Well, as much as this freedom from thinking felt good, it was short lived. But this is not at all surprising since it was, in fact, imposed upon me from an outside source instead of being an inner conscious decision.

> *The only way to learn how to think is by FIRST learning how NOT to think,*
> *just as you have to get your hands off the keyboard if you want a teacher to show you how to play the piano.*

The Gaza Strip Was Quite A Tease

Once the basic training was over, I was stationed in Gaza. It was a horrible place and also the most dangerous location in Israel at that time. I could not go home very often due to the frequent hand grenade explosions that occurred between the base and the main land. In fact, a car I was in did get attacked once by a hand grenade that blew up an inch from where I was sitting. It is a miracle I am still here. So, you just never knew if you would get home alive.

As depressing as this was, a ray of hope emerged when my father gave me the book *Siddhartha* by Hermann Hesse, that deals with the spiritual journey of a young man during the time of the Buddha. I could not put the book down. Every evening I would gather the other base-bound soldiers in my dorm and, sitting on my bunk bed, I would read to them page after page with great enthusiasm.

Although this became my new source of joy, it also rekindled my longing for freedom and awakened within me an intense yearning for love and self-realization. Yet here I was, locked up in a war zone; therein lies the tease.

> *"I have had to experience so much stupidity,*
> *so many vices, so much error, so much nausea,*
> *disillusionment and sorrow, just in order to*
> *become a child again and begin anew."*
> *– Hermann Hesse, Siddhartha*

Little did I know that the above statement would become the story of my life. My yearning soon turned into frustration and before I knew it, I was drinking a bottle of Vermouth every evening. I had to get drunk to alleviate this pain. I was also experiencing a deep disappointment in love as a result of my parents' ugly divorce, and my own relationships, that produced nothing but hurt and anguish.

One day I took off and hitchhiked to the Wailing Wall in Jerusalem, where people write their prayers and wishes on little pieces of paper and stick them in the cracks between the huge wall stones. On my little paper I wrote, "I want to find true love, divine love, the love of God that is pure, unchanging and everlasting."

Yippy! I Am Now A Hippie

When my army days were over, I would have been accepted to any university since I graduated from high school with very good grades. However, my inner itch for finding God or self-realization was still so strong that I refused to enroll, or start anything for that matter, that didn't absolutely grab me and promise to be the answer to my quest.

And so for the time being I gave up drinking and I took up the life of a hippie, dabbling in hash, LSD, magic mushrooms and everything else that went with it. I moved into a commune of artists and musicians with my new boyfriend, who was an actor and a drummer, and with whom I fell in love on an "acid trip." We were all blissed out on the highs of drugs and the marvels of hallucinations accompanied by the constant self-inquiry, "Who the hell am I?" And, of course, there were also the nasty lows that followed the highs. We were desperately trying to develop a new identity by naming ourselves "freaks" and by calling everyone else a "square." This lifestyle was to represent my new freedom.

One night a strange thing happened in my sleep. I became totally aware, even though everything around me disappeared. A pitch black void enveloped me. I could feel an intense and tangible presence, yet not with the regular senses. I asked what this was, but not with words. The nonverbal response was, "I am the power of love. And all that is ever needed is love." I was utterly startled by this and told no one.

Within a few weeks my boyfriend and I broke up and the commune we lived in dissolved. By now the overwhelming thirst for truth, God, knowledge, or anything that could offer me some kind of liberation became almost unbearable.

I found myself visiting a friend whose library of spiritual books covered an entire wall in his living room. Every conceivable new age book by any spiritual teacher was there, from Baba Ram Dass to Ramtha and then some. I literally looked through all the books, only to find each one of them too intellectual for my taste. In my great disappointment I said my good-byes and was ready to leave.

On my way out I stepped into the washroom and there on the floor were two books by Swami Muktananda. I picked them up and noticed that one had a picture of the swami inside. His eyes were so full of love that I was almost knocked over. Underneath the picture there were the words, "There is boundless love within. Go there and find it."

I instantly knew that this was my new direction, the fulfillment of the wondrous experience I had with the presence of love. My friend told me that these books were mailed to him from India by an American mutual friend of ours who was now living in this swami's ashram. Oddly enough, this friend's name was Israel. I took the books home and, without even reading them, I immediately wrote a letter to our friend, Israel. I asked him if he thought I was crazy for having this firm resolve and determination to go to India, to that swami's ashram, after just seeing his picture.

Israel's reply was a great relief. He wrote that it was not so unusual to have such a response when seeing the picture of his Guru, whom he called Baba, a term of endearment, meaning father. He also said that it was customary to bring a present for Baba and suggested that a yarmulke (Jewish cap) would be a good idea, since I was coming from Israel and because Baba loved to wear hats.

He warned me, however, not to be upset if Baba would immediately give my gift away. After all, Baba lived a life of renunciation and didn't hang on to anything that was given to him. Israel also recommended that I quit eating meat, since the ashram food was strictly vegetarian. And so, from that moment, I gave up meat, eggs, coffee, cigarettes, alcohol and all drugs, cold turkey.

Where There Is A Will, There Are Opposing Friends And Relatives

The opposition that confronted me, as a result of my decision, was overwhelming. After all, I was only 22 and I had never travelled alone. My father was enraged. He would have been much happier if I were to continue with the drugs instead of pursuing the crazy idea of going to India. He sent me to a psychologist in an attempt to change my course of action. After speaking with her, the psychologist told my father that I was in the right frame of mind, and asked what was wrong with him.

Then my father tried to bribe me to stay by offering to pay for my entire higher education, but that did not work either. So finally, he resorted to using the good old scare tactic; he had his ex-girlfriend talk to me about the horrors she witnessed when she was in India, which included rape, robbery and murder. I listened patiently to her frightening accounts but I knew in my heart that this was a movement towards God and if I didn't go, there was no point in living anyway. My attitude was, that if I had to die by going to India, then so be it. At least I would have tried my utmost to find my Creator.

My stepmother jumped on the disapproval bandwagon and offered me a large sum of money to buy a house. When my parents got divorced my birth mother was in such a poor mental state that my father put 25% of our fully paid off three-bedroom house in my name in order to protect me from being thrown out. When my mother recovered and sold the house I got my share, and now my step mother was offering to match my early inheritance so that I could purchase my own home on the condition, of course, that I cancel my trip to India. Needless to say, her generous suggestion fell on deaf ears.

Then came the ex-boyfriend's turn. He showed up every day asking me to stay in Israel and marry him. I had longed for him to propose to me for quite some time, but all I could say at this point was that he would have to meet me in India if he ever wanted to see me again. Another friend offered to take me on a trip around the world, all expenses paid. But nothing and no one could stop me!

Amazing that as soon as I made that first major decision in my life, I could have had a house, a trip around the world, all my tuition paid for and the husband of my dreams, all to lure me away from my heart's desire and keep me chained to conventional living. But I guess when intuition strikes, worldly temptations and acquisitions seem to lose their appeal and even the secure feeling of a familiar comfort zone begins to fade into oblivion. Within three weeks I was on the plane to India with my entire early inheritance and a little black velvet yarmulke that I spent hours embroidering for Baba.

Gold chains are still chains.

Chapter Two

FIRST DECEPTION: WHAT WILL IT TAKE TO EARN MY BIRTHRIGHT?

My First Steps On The Dead-End Spiritual Road

I arrived in India at a perfect time. The monsoon season was finally over and everything was lush and green. My excitement knew no end! I could hardly wait to finally meet my Guru, the man whom I already believed was going to help me find God or self-realization. It was a lofty goal, but now I was well on my way and my spiritual drive was gaining momentum like a raging river.

At Baba's request, Israel (the person) kept me in Bombay for one day before travelling to the ashram in order to assist me in buying some clothes that were more suitable for ashram life. I guess my hippie wardrobe, which consisted of ripped jeans with huge eagles embroidered on them and tie-dye see-through tank tops, was not going to cut it.

The next day off we went to the ashram on a train that was so packed I thought people would fall off, and then a bus that was just as crammed. Yes, I saw the poverty on the way in the small villages and men taking their morning shit on the side of the road and yes, the bus reeked of human sweat, smoked hair from outdoor cooking, and raw fish. But none of that bothered me in the least. I was going to meet my Guru and all was right with the world.

When we arrived at the ashram, lunch had already begun. I was rushed into the huge dining room where everyone was sitting cross legged on long red runners spread horizontally in parallel rows on a concrete floor. The men sat on one side of the hall and women on the other. Everyone ate in silence using their right hand. There were no utensils.

I later learned that the left hand was only to be used in the washroom after relieving oneself and by relieving oneself, I don't mean sitting on a nice porcelain toilet and using scented, soft toilet paper. I am talking about squatting and doing your business into a hole and then washing yourself with water which came from a tiny tap near the floor. So, believe me, you would not want to be caught eating with your left hand in the ashram. I felt really bad for the left-handed people.

But I digress. The only eye contact I observed in that dining room was when Indian servers came rushing around dumping food on the disciples' plates which were made of dried grape leaves stitched together. This was the time to let the servers know how much or how little of the food you wanted by making a quick hand gesture. Being a man, Israel went to sit down on the men's side and handed me over to a couple of ladies who showed me where to sit and eat. Some food was already placed on a grape-leaf plate for me in anticipation of my slightly late arrival.

The only thing I recognized on the plate was the white rice and the flat bread that looked a bit like a pita. There was also some kind of soup and a mixture of vegetables, of which only few were vaguely familiar to me. Being quite hungry I dove right in. Holy shit, was that ever hot! My mouth was burning, my nose was running and my mascara was making marks on my cheeks. So I resolved to stick with the rice and bread. I noticed that people who finished eating were taking their used leaves and dumping them into a huge outdoor concrete garbage pit, where they were thrown away after the crows have had their crack at them.

I carefully gathered my flimsy plate with the left over "hot stuff" and did what everyone else did with theirs. Before I could turn around from the garbage pit an older Indian lady, dressed like a monk in an orange sari, glared at me with intense rage and began to scold me. "How dare you throw away food in an ashram? This is a terrible sin and I am sure that now Baba is furious with you."

I would have loved to explain that the servers put that food on my plate without my knowledge of what it was but my shock of learning that the Guru, whom I had yet to meet, was now livid because of this horrendous faux pas stopped me in my tracks. When the ability to speak resumed, I apologised profusely and began to make my way out of the dining room, not really knowing where to go.

Suddenly an old Indian man came rushing to me. He had a beautiful smile, bright shiny eyes, and he spoke through a handkerchief-covered hole located at the front of his neck, since he was a cancer survivor. I could barely make out what he was saying. Somehow I picked up that he was very eager to escort me to meet Baba. As I followed this sweet old man, his warm and loving disposition, in contrast to my previous encounter in the dining room, greatly eased my trepidation.

And there was Baba. He was sitting like a king on a raised marble platform in front of his apartment overlooking a majestic courtyard. He was wearing a silk orange lungi (a traditional men's garment worn in India), a shawl, a hat and sunglasses. I was told that he wore sunglasses around people so that his intense penetrating gaze wouldn't startle them (or was he really hiding behind them?). There were several devotees around him, gawking at him with syrupy smiles. Some people were approaching and bowing before him, while others were sitting on the spotless marble floor in deep admiration or lost in meditation. Oddly enough, most of the people were Westerners.

The air was filled with the fragrance of incense mixed with the scent of blooming local flowers. Not one thing was familiar to me and there was no way I could have ever imagined what this place and experience would be like. I had no reference point to match any of what my senses were taking in. My eyes quickly scouted the area looking for Israel (the man), the only person I knew, but he was nowhere to be found.

When Baba noticed me, he motioned to me to come closer. Someone whispered to me that it was customary to bow before Baba but if I was not comfortable with this it would be acceptable not to do so at this point. I walked up towards Baba and, being the go-getter I was, I decided to give the "bowing" thing a try. It was a bit awkward but somehow I got through it. There was an Indian interpreter by Baba's side who introduced me.

"Where are you from?" Baba asked.

"Israel," I replied.

"Who brought you here?" he continued.

"Israel" was my answer.

"Ah! Whatever I ask her, she says 'Israel'" he commented with a twinkle in his well concealed eyes.

That bit of comic relief was enough to put me at ease and fortunately I remembered to give him the yarmulke. To my great amazement, and to my ego's delight, he took off the hat he was wearing and put on the yarmulke. I later found out that he actually kept it for three whole days, which was longer than he held on to most gifts he received.

And there it was, the first tiny bud of my blossoming spiritual ego. Little did I know that while I thought my journey to self-realization was just beginning, it actually came to a screeching dead-end halt. I was now being put to sleep by the spiritual awakening of my ego which was carefully watching and scrutinizing everything, just like an enemy who observes every move of its opponent so that it could strike first.

And then the other shoe fell as Baba's powerful yet seemingly compassionate and all-knowing gaze sneaked through his sunglasses on to me and in his authoritative yet divinatory voice he proclaimed, "One day you will realize that you are Jesus Christ." Yes, it seemed a bit odd to me at first, since I just gave him a yarmulke, and I knew about Jesus as much as I knew about Henry XIV. However, it barely took a nanosecond for my ego to come to full bloom and grace me with the angelic bliss of feeling so very special.

Now my goose was cooked. From this point on, my soul's sincere quest to reunite with its Source was slowly but surely being soiled by the ego/mind that took charge in leading the way to enlightenment. I was not the least bit aware of this. Lucky for the ego, it knows exactly how to conceal itself and with great skill and dexterity it was capable of remaining totally invisible to my unaware eye/I for a long time.

> *A spiritual ego is already immunized against*
> *the possibility of awakening.*
> *A regular ego still has hope.*

The New Frontier, Where No Wimp Has Ever Gone Before

It was the early 70s and Baba had recently returned from his first world tour. There were mostly American people living in the ashram, plus one or two French, Danish, Swedish, Australian, and I was the only Israeli. The lifestyle and discipline were quite stark.

There was a dormitory for men and one for the women. Even the married couples (of which there were only three at that time) had to live separately in their respective dorms. There were also separate residences for Indians and for Westerners. The one I was in had about 50 wooden cots with hay-filled mattresses and they were lined up about a foot apart from each other. There was no other furniture and the only décor was the few very large pictures of Baba and his Guru hanging on the walls. All my belongings were to be placed in a straw basket that had to fit neatly under my bed. I had very few clothes so it was not a problem.

All the women wore saris, which took a while to learn how to put on. Since there were no irons or ironing boards we had to spread the saris between the cot and the mattress at night so that in the morning they wouldn't look wrinkled. Very few beds were positioned by a window so if you were fortunate enough to have a "window-bed" it was only because you were there long enough to have earned it. There was no talking in the dorms and, needless to say, there were no TVs, radios, newspapers nor any books, other than the ones written by Baba.

The wake up bell went off at 3 a.m. at which point everyone had to make their way in the dark to the bath stalls. It was about a three-minute walk through the courtyard and a garden and, of course, we had to watch out for scorpions since no shoes were allowed in the ashram. All shoes were taken off and left at the gate that was locked up at night. The bath stalls were nothing but a stone floor with a drain and a couple of eye level concrete walls. Each person got a half a bucket of water (not always warm) and a plastic mug to fetch the water from the bucket and pour it on the body. If you needed to wash your clothes, you got an extra half a bucket of water.

After the bath, everyone headed to the meditation room and found their way in the dark to a cushion on the floor where they sat for meditation. During meditation Baba would sometimes walk around with his bright flashlight which he would occasionally shine on people's faces to ensure their heads were not dangling in "sleepetation." Those who were trying really hard to meditate often thought they were having visions of bright light, not realizing it was Baba's flashlight.

The bell rang again at 5 a.m. for the Guru Gita chant at which point all the meditators silently got up and trailed into the huge temple. This was a one-and-a-half hour long chant in Sanskrit in praise of the Guru. While chanting with full voice and using our diaphragms, we had to maintain an erect sitting position and hold our text books up in front of our noses. Baba often joined us, sitting on a velvet throne, hollering insults at anyone who looked like they were dozing off, and occasionally throwing his book at a sleepy chanter.

After the chant we usually got a cup of "gun-powder" chai and then went to fulfill our work assignments, usually cleaning, working in the garden or helping in the kitchen. There was no breakfast. Those who needed to eat something in the morning went out to a nearby café, but it was not looked upon as a very spiritual thing to do so naturally, I never went out. Before lunch there was another chant and after lunch you could either go back to your chores or attend another chant and then go to work. Before supper there was another chant and after dinner – you got it - another chant. Lights went out at 9 p.m.

All these events and activities were mandatory. There was no socializing whatsoever. There was no disobeying or skipping any scheduled activity no matter what. If you were sick, you had to leave the ashram and spend time in Bombay at some devotee's house till you could resume the full ashram program. For most people this routine was quite difficult and several left after a few days. Baba used to say that he never had to kick anyone out. They would leave on their own if they couldn't handle the discipline. Having been in the Israeli army, the life in the ashram was not so hard for me to handle. I also was not bothered by the summer's scorching heat, since I was used to hot climate.

Waiting For God...Oh!

Twice a week Baba spoke in the temple. It was a satsang where he answered questions that were submitted prior to the session and read to him by his translator. He was charming and very entertaining. He didn't always offer the exact answer to what was asked but it was common knowledge that, since the Guru was all-knowing, his replies were always what the disciples needed to hear no matter what they intended to ask.

Besides the books that I found at my friend's house in Israel, Baba also published his spiritual autobiography called The Play of Consciousness, which was considered to be the most important book of all. This volume delineates all the steps and experiences that a disciple of his would have to go through by using as a blueprint the detailed descriptions of his own experiences. These encounters included everything from the dramatic initiation he received from his Guru, his Kundalini awakening, years of meditation in solitude accompanied by inner struggles, a myriad of visions, unusual physical movements, astral travels to other realms unseen, and then the ultimate grand vision and explosive event which he concluded was his final self-realization.

The invisible bar was set very high and the cheese at the end was very tantalizing, so little did I realize how seductive all this was. I see now how easy it was to fall into such a trap. I was so wrapped up in this spiritual fantasy that I never even stopped to question why I would base my union with the source on another's past experience with a hope for a non-existent future.

Today I call this "spiritual hearsay" that guarantees one will not pay any attention to the present moment nor to the discovery element of one's own unique evolution. Furthermore, the more dramatic and grandiose the "hearsay" is, the more unattainable it seems to us "little spiritual people" and yet, somehow, the ego's drive to chase after this lofty, impressive and elusive goal starts to grow out of proportion.

Baba's motto was, "Honor yourself and kneel to your own self, because God dwells within you as you." He also expressed the great truth that what we were seeking was never lost. All this sounded fantastic. Oh, but wait. Initially you have to worship the Guru with all you've got. The Guru is a representative of God. So, if you ever want to realize the God of you, yes, the one that is already inside you and has been all along, the one whom it's your birthright to know and be but you haven't got a clue what that is other than your current deluded identity that you spent your life creating in your head, if that's what you want to attain, well, sorry, you must first obey, please and basically spend years sucking up to the supreme Guru until he finds you worthy enough to bestow his grace upon you.

And this is exactly what I was striving to do, with a Guru who kept us motivated with Kundalini awakenings so that we could have all kinds of wonderful spiritual experiences on a psychic level and be fooled into believing that we were making progress on the path. After all, these were very dazzling sign posts. Oh, he did tell us that they were in fact sign posts and that we didn't really need them, but his autobiography was full of vivid descriptions of these experiences that, apparently, led him to realization, so....

Well, congratulations, fellow seekers. We have just been initiated into the great mystical teachings of "partial truths." Since there are a couple of true statements, we buy into the whole spiel just as we do when a psychic nails one true piece of information out of a hundred. She accidentally hits one of our reference points and we believe that everything she says from that point on is accurate.

> *Psychic: Do you have an aunt in New York?*
> *Client: No*
> *Psychic: Was your dog's name fluffy?*
> *Client: No*
> *Psychic: Did your grandma have false teeth?*
> *Client: Wow, yes! Maybe I do have an aunt in New York?*
> *Maybe in a past life my dog's name was fluffy?*

So good luck getting out of the maze in which your Kundalini is cleaning out your chakras from the past while you are locked into an obscure and elusive, yet highly exciting future event, a trap that is designed to develop your spiritual ego to the point of (almost) no return. Now you have finally reached the status of a mouse running on its wheel, searching for your ever-present inner God; anytime but now and anywhere but inside.

You might believe you are doing inner work since you are meditating, having visions and all kinds of emotions and, after all, you are completely dedicated to cultivating the behavior of a spiritual recluse, renouncing anything you can think of so that you may appear to have transcended the body and the senses. However, these are all done with the mind that has now ensnared you into a spiritual identity, and your so called achievements are fleeting at best in spite of the sporadic moments of bliss that keep you from realizing what is really going on. Well, since you seem to be happy some of the time, you must be on the right track.

Without realizing it, you are now "doing" your spiritual life, just as you did with your previous worldly time-based life:

"When I finish high school and all these exams, I will be free."

"Oh shit, now there's the army. Ok, when that's over, my life will be in order."

"When my Uranus stops squaring my Venus, I will at last be in control of my love-life."

And finally, "When the Guru is pleased, I will finally be enlightened."

Now that we have added the "Guru's grace" component, we have something else outside of ourselves to add to the mix of things we rely and depend upon:

"By the Guru's grace, I might become a monk and a great teacher and reach the height of my spiritual career."

"By the Guru's grace, I will get a good job or a better spouse."

And on and on it goes in the deep sleep of being stuck in bliss.

> *"So Mendel, how do you like your new job*
> *as the lookout who waits on a hill for the Messiah?"*
> *"Well, Rabbi, it doesn't pay much,*
> *but at least I am guaranteed job security."*

Occasionally Baba would read, narrate a story, or recite a poem from some other Indian guru or poet saint, but only if those great beings were already dead and/or out of reach. Others, like Osho, whom today I admire, were bad-mouthed severely and the ashram library was careful to carry only those books that Baba approved of. He often warned us to stay away from bad company which comprised of anyone who was not totally devoted to the path that he paved for us. So now, not only was my Guru secure in his profession, since his disciples' egos were well on their way to an everlasting and mesmerizing impossible goal, but he had also eliminated the threat of competition. Man, am I ever in the wrong business.

Kundalini Awakening – The End Of My Spiritual Virginity

My initial intent was to stay in the ashram for a few months and after that, I would head to Canada. But then the great event happened. My Kundalini was awakened. I must have done something right in a past incarnation. It took place on a glorious night, the full moon in September, just a week after my arrival. I was told that all these signs were very significant and I bought that, of course, hook line and sinker.

Now I felt even more special. I did not have to wait for months or years for this to transpire. Such grace! It occurred in the middle of the evening chant when suddenly I felt a bolt of energy surge up my spine from the very base to the top of my head, where it felt like an explosion had gone off. Wow. My whole body trembled in ecstasy and began to sway. My heart chakra flung wide open and I was sobbing and laughing uncontrollably. I also had a high fever for three days, which I was told was a good thing since it indicated a cleansing of my chakras.

This sealed the deal for me. I decided there and then that the ashram was my new home and that I would stay indefinitely. Now that I had this initiation, all I could think about was how and what I should do to please my Guru in order to achieve the final realization as he did, as soon as possible. This turned into an ambition and an obsession. I felt that if I gave myself completely to him, I would get God in return. Why wouldn't I think that? Most of the stories Baba told had that very same message.

So instead of waking up at 3 a.m. I often got up at 2 a.m. and started sewing things for Baba by candle light in some hidden place. At times I skipped meditation in the morning since that felt like something I was doing for myself and instead, I found some work I could do for him. I would stand in front of his picture for hours crying my eyes out and begging him to deliver me, or kill me.

Looking back, I can't believe some of the ways I tried to get into Baba's good graces and, of course, this also turned into a quest for attention which inflated my competitive nature without my ever detecting it. So, you tell me, who was "doing" the path? My ego or my soul? Was this really a homecoming? Or a desperate attempt to prove myself, and keep my mind busy by being on a "search?"

> *So many people are led to believe that kundalini awaking is essential. What is essential is that we wake up and leave the poor kundalini alone. Allow the intelligence of your body to decide if and when you need it. Having the kundalini experience as a pre-requisite is just another mind trick to keep you excited, motivated and confident in your spiritual progress. It is nothing but mental stimulation to keep you enchanted with your search for what you already are. The ever-existing Silence of Being does not depend on kundalini awakening any more than a stallion needs Viagra.*

No Mo' Money, No Mo' Honey

One very early morning I sewed a silk pouch for Baba so that he could put the pens and mantra cards, that he kept by him, into it. When it was completed, I went up to where he was sitting and gave it to him. As he took it from me he asked if he could put money in it. Without hesitation I went straight to the bank next door and took all my money out of my safe. I then went up to Baba again and handed him a fist full of all the inheritance I had left. I did not even leave a cent for basic necessities, or for a ticket back home, should I ever need to leave. Baba reached over to open the door to his apartment and, while still remaining seated, he casually threw the money in, closing the door behind it.

During one of the satsang sessions with Baba, a question was asked about marriage by a young couple who wished to get married. In his reply, Baba was very much against it, claiming that marriage was a terrible distraction for one who was attempting to live a full ashram life. He advocated celibacy so that the Kundalini energy would not be wasted by the frivolous activity of sex. Baba referred to sex as "two bodies rubbing against each other" and disrespectfully maintained that, "Even animals do it, so what's the big deal?"

From that point on I swore off sex and decided to become a monk, a swami. I wore only orange saris and put on a red dot between my eyebrows every morning. I wrote to my ex-boyfriend, who was about to come to see me, telling him I will never get married and that he would be wasting his time and money if he came. In his disbelief, a few weeks later he showed up nonetheless. Much to his dismay, he found a fanatic devotee working or chanting every waking moment. And so my not-so-long-lost honey freaked out and left after two days.

How To Lose Your Dad In Record Time

One night I got a phone call from my dad in Israel. The connection was so bad that he sent me an express letter (no emails at that time, let alone Skype) begging me to come and meet him in Italy for one week, all expenses on him. He promised to take me all around Italy and then send me back to the ashram, no questions asked.

I replied to his letter by stating that what I found in India was so important to me that I couldn't bear the thought of leaving even for one day. To my great astonishment and delight this had a great effect on him.

He immediately wrote back saying, "The fact that you found something that means so much to you makes me very proud and impressed. So much so that I am planning to come to visit you at your ashram."

Needless to say, I was overjoyed, excited beyond words, and up for the challenge. This was really good news. I always felt that my father was more of an outside the box kind of person, being an artist and all, and now to have him share with me my newfound love, how wonderful could that be? But alas, my thrill was not only short lived but actually turned into a huge disappointment.

In preparation for his arrival, I decided to record on tape all the events of the day, the 3 a.m. meditation, the chants, following the Guru to the garden and watching him feed the elephant; you know, the usual stuff that any parent would get excited about. Nope, not my dad. After listening to the recording I sent, I got the final letter from him in which he declared I was no longer his daughter. Amazing how low the pendulum can swing after such a high.

Nevertheless, there is always a silver lining in the realm of the mind. I was now able to decorate myself with yet another spiritual accolade; I chose God over my father. My pride helped to ease, or rather to suppress, the pain of losing my dear old friend, my worldly Baba. Looking back, I can now see the role that my ego played in softening the blow of being abandoned by my dad instead of allowing me to use this shock to transcend the ups and downs of life and the vacillations of duality.

"A shock is life's way of telling us that we have swung too far away from our Original Being." – Gabor

---

You Lose Some, You Win Some, Your Ego Is On The Loose Some

One day Baba summoned me to the inner sanctum of the meditation room, which was part of his apartment. The two minutes it took to get there seemed like an hour. I was a wreck. "Did I do something wrong? Is he going to scold me?" was all I could think about. I loved Baba very much and I was also terrified of displeasing him. I could not afford to be cut off from "his" grace.

When I got there, he was sitting on one of his beautiful thrones waiting for me. I kneeled before him and touched his feet, scared to raise my head.

Suddenly I felt something being wrapped around my shoulders. Lo and behold, it was a huge, orange, crushed velvet shawl embroidered in gold that used to be draped around his Guru's statue. I was extremely moved and honored to receive such a gift. Now my ego was soaring to brand new heights. I felt that Baba really *did* notice how devoted I was to him. Ahhh, the bliss of being recognized and approved.

A few days later Baba put the cherry on my egoic cake by giving me a new name, Bhakti-bai, which means devotion. Yes, I was his at last. I surrendered to my Guru and surely, by now, I must be worthy of, what? What was it that I really wanted? The ego was so pleased with its accomplishment and with my new identity I almost forgot what prompted me to embark on this path in the first place.

Looking back, I remember hearing Baba say that the Guru's job is to devour the disciple's ego. Somehow, this was definitely not happening in my case. I now know that no one, not even King Shit, can remove another's ego. It is an "inside" job and as long as we haven't entered the real inner realm the job ain't getting done, no matter how hard the ego tries to pretend it is being eradicated.

> **Asking the ego to protect you from your ego**
> **is like asking a goat to guard your cabbage.**

But somehow, something was still missing. "What more could I do?" "There are some people who might be working harder, I have to do better." "Perhaps some heavy duty labour would be good?" As these endless thoughts were gnawing at me, I was sent to work in the ashram's rose garden.

Who Killed The Roses?

The rose garden was a large plot with several statues of Indian saints and gurus, including Baba's statue and his guru's statue. I was put in charge of the garden and my mandate was to plant roses of different colours around each statue. The problem was that, in addition to my not-so-green thumb,

I knew nothing about planting roses or how to care for them. Apparently, there is a whole science behind this and the girl who took care of the garden before me was so crushed to have been replaced that she refused to share her vast knowledge.

To make things worse, a hot-headed French girl showed up a few days later claiming that Baba put her in charge of the rose garden. She too knew nothing about roses. We were told that roses needed to be in a pleasant environment and to be spoken to daily in a loving and admiring tone. Unfortunately, with each one of us demanding to be "in charge" and our inability to agree on anything, the rose garden turned into an ego war zone. Instead of being showered with praise, the poor roses had to witness our argumentative blood baths. Evidently, this was Baba's way of having us work on one another's ego.

Well, I guess I pissed this girl's French temper so much that she took off and I was left all alone to dig 90 ditches in the heat of the Indian summer in preparation for the arrival of new roses from Delhi. I worked so hard and for such long hours that just before the roses arrived I became terribly ill and was not available to handle, or even to supervise, the "semi-proper" planting of the roses. Naturally, all the roses died.

As I lay in bed I began to wonder what went wrong with my plan. It never even occurred to me that everything I was doing was orchestrated by my relentless ego, which considered enlightenment to be its ultimate conquest.

Why Are Non-Spiritual People So Much Nicer?

Baba instilled in us the discipline of restricting our circle of acquaintances to those who were on the same path. For many years I did not have the privilege of choosing who I associated with, since I lived in ashrams and meditation centers and was always surrounded by a group of devotees or students who were involved in the same teaching as I was. Back in the day, I so admired people who had a strong longing for God.

Today, however, my experience is that the best friends that I have, and the nicest people I know, are ones who are not spiritual at all. My guess is that they have not been contaminated by the mind's attempt to develop a spiritual ego, which only fosters separation; "I am more spiritually advance than she is" or "I have a better Guru than they have." No wonder these types of disciples, as I was, have such an intense pining for God. The more the ego and mind are involved, the further away we feel from God and the so called "others."

> *A disciple was travelling with his Guru. Upon arriving at the gates of a large kingdom, the Guru warned him not to say anything about himself when interrogated by the guards. The Guru was first to be questioned, but he remained silent with an empty gaze. He was instantly ushered in, as he appeared to be more of a "nut" than a threat. The disciple, on the other hand, began to brag: "I am a great devotee of the famous Guru Beyondananda. Don't your recognize him? I have been with him for many years. I am a very spiritual person." The poor dude was beaten to a pulp and kicked out.*

So yes, we were told to drop the ego, but how does the ego do away with the ego? It's like asking Billy, the goat, to guard the cabbage. We were encouraged to cultivate the behavior of a modest follower of truth, but when the ego is leading on the path one encounters nothing but endless failed efforts and short lived attempts to mimic the behavior and attitudes of someone we assume has united with the innate presence in all beings. This becomes an ever growing vortex and it keeps us spinning further and further away from our very own birth right.

The Wheels On The Spiritual Bus Go Round And Round

Towards the end of my second year in the ashram, Baba was preparing to go on his second world tour. As part of this plan he had a big sanyasi ceremony conducted for several disciples whom he had selected to be initiated into the Paramahansa order of swamis, to which he belonged. These monks were to travel with him and assist him as lecturers in his various centers around the world. I so longed to become a swami as well, but this option was not open to me at this point so I resigned to continue to live as a monk until Baba would choose to initiate me.

Nonetheless, there was a very special feeling about the whole event so with great admiration, I approached one of the initiates and asked, "Tell me, what is it like? How does it feel to become a swami?" Her reply nearly knocked my sari off. "This is great," she said, "It is the next step in my spiritual career."

I didn't know how to respond to that. For me, taking this oath of monkhood was a symbol of giving oneself completely to the teachings, dissolving the ego, and merging with the divine. I never considered it as a "career" move.

Many other Western devotees were getting ready to accompany Baba on his tour. I would have loved to go too, but I had no money left. "I don't need to go," I thought to myself. "I can stay here and do his work by looking after the ashram that I have come to love and adore." Little did I realize that once he left, there was not much to do. "Well," I continued my inner talk, "Why don't I go back to Israel and open a meditation center there? I could translate Baba's books and teach what I have learned." This felt so right, like intuition speaking again. So I wrote a letter to Baba, who was now somewhere in the U.S., asking him for permission to put this idea into motion.

Weeks went by and there was no reply. Patience was never one of my virtues. One day I overheard one of the ashram's trustees saying that he was going to call Baba on the phone that night. I asked him if he would kindly ask Baba for a reply to my question. The next morning I got my answer. Baba said it was fine to go and start a center in Israel. I was over the moon. Of course, I had no money to buy a ticket but somehow, out of the blue, the fellow I borrowed Baba's books from remembered that he owed me some money and without my asking for it, he sent it just at the right time. Was it a sign? Who the hell knows?

I bought my ticket and was getting ready to leave, but not without mixed feelings. I loved the ashram that had become my new home and yet I looked forward to my new project. Since I had a late evening flight I was invited to spend the day in Bombay with a family of devotees who knew Baba for many years. In fact, the first two of the four children grew up very close to Baba and were later to become his successors. I was so honored to be invited to their home and, of course, accepted the invitation.

That whole day I was shown family pictures, and I was overwhelmed by seeing that Baba was in every one of them. I couldn't help feeling how wonderful it must be to know the Guru so intimately and to start the spiritual journey from the first day of one's life. What a great way to grow up!

You Can Take The Girl Out Of The Ashram, But Not The Ashram Out Of The Girl

Coming back to Israel softened my father for a short while. Through his contacts, I found a beautiful Arabic style apartment in the old city of Jaffa, which had thick whitewashed stone walls and high arched ceilings. I picked it since the large living room was the perfect size and structure for starting my first mediation center. I had no furniture there, only meditation cushions and an altar where I placed Baba's slippers, a statue of Baba's Guru and plenty of incense and candles. The walls were covered with huge pictures of Baba.

I lived there just as I did in the ashram, maintaining all the chants from 5 a.m. to the last evening chant. At home I continued to wear an orange sari, as I was still hoping to become a monk someday. Since I had no profession or any particular skill, I got a job cleaning the home of an orthodox Jewish family.

This was a filthy rich family. They owned several hotels in Tel Aviv yet lived in a small apartment with their seven children. Needless to say, they were not big spenders. My rent and my monthly salary were exactly the same so I had to babysit a few evenings a week in order to buy food, candles and incense. I was so poor, my diet mostly consisted of bread and margarine. I couldn't afford an umbrella so I ordered God to have it rain only when I was indoors and, for the most part, He cooperated.

Somehow, between my cleaning job, babysitting and running the center, I found time to translate Baba's book, The Play of Consciousness, into Hebrew. People started to come to the center and bring their friends. I held satsang several times a week, and a Saturday morning chant. The acoustics were so good that when the chanting went on, the walls would echo and vibrate with our booming voices.

Unfortunately, my apartment/center was next door to my father's house, and hearing the chanting that went on at all hours drove him crazy, as did the large pictures of Baba hanging on every wall. Oh, and I guess telling him that I was planning to be a monk for the rest of my life didn't help much. Once again, he would have nothing to do with me, and he also threatened to sue Baba for brainwashing his little girl.

However, my dreams of becoming a swami were soon shattered. News from the U.S. came via the ashram's monthly newsletter that Baba was now performing marriage ceremonies in the West. It seemed as though he was trying to make his teachings more suitable to the Western culture and was now preaching, "Be in the world, but not of the world."

I was becoming quite confused, especially when seeing the beautiful, happy Indian wedding pictures which Baba presided over that were featured in the newsletters. Some of the brides in those photos were good friends of mine whom I had admired very much and even looked up to when I was in India. "So now what?" I wondered. "How do I fit in this picture?"

> *"Being in the world but not of the world.*
> *For one who has entered the inner kingdom and has*
> *transcended the 3rd dimension, it is both an accurate*
> *statement and an obvious one. Otherwise, it is a meaningless*
> *concept, since it has been overused, bastardized and stained by*
> *the mind." – Gabor*

The concept of being single, and especially a monk, was not so easy to do away with. Who knows for how many lifetimes I had been carrying that burden with me? But no matter what the belief is, trying to overcome it with the mind never works. I see now more than ever how complex the ego is and how it tries everything and anything to keep its story alive. My new incessant nagging – "Should I stick to the romantic notion of becoming a monk, or would it be better to renounce it, for the sake of blending with the new fad?" – was my ego's way of making sure that my mind was well fed and its survival was secure.

Well, wouldn't you know it. A temporary relief manifested and the decision was "kinda" made for me. I fell in love with one of the devotees who had been coming to my center for a year and who had been very supportive. With Baba's permission I got married. It was all very exciting.

My father figured that now I would surely be normal. He not only made up with me but he threw a fabulous wedding for us outdoors by the light house in the old city of Jaffa and a beautiful reception in his home/gallery in the artist colony that he helped to establish. We then had a Yemeni wedding at the home of my new in-laws. After that we flew to Oakland, California, for a month, where my new husband finally met Baba and where Baba performed an Indian wedding for us along with eight other couples.

On that trip I found out that I was pregnant. When my father heard this news, he sent telegrams to his friends all over the world announcing that he was about to become a grandfather. He invited my husband and me for dinner immediately after our return back to Israel. But what he discovered at that last supper with us shattered his joy and hopes of ever having a "normal" daughter. Not only did my marriage not change me in the least but my husband was just as "crazy" and into the "Indian" stuff as I was and totally committed to this weird path. This was the last straw for my father and from that day I never saw him again. He didn't even want to meet my child.

The Saga Continues In The Land Of Guilt And Honey

What can I say? As long as we are still in the mind, no matter how spiritual we "think" we are, we can never be free of the ups and downs or the highs and lows of life. There is no stability or peace when the mind is guiding us. The fact that my father dis-owned me and dis-inherited me for the last time was quite a blow, even though I was starting to get used to the tantrums he threw when he couldn't be in control. But even worse than that was the deep and penetrating sense of guilt that was gnawing at me for having abandoned my aspiration to becoming a monk.

My three big fat "Jewish-Yemeni-Indian" weddings were over, the trip to California and seeing Baba again ended, and in an instant, as if out of nowhere, the feelings of "what have I done?" took center stage. I felt that I had betrayed my Guru by giving a part of myself to someone else. My devotion now had to be split and could no longer be focused on God alone. But there was no going back; I was very pregnant. My only comfort was that my child would be able to grow up in a spiritual environment and with a Guru from day one, just like Baba's future successors whom I had seen in the family photo album before leaving India.

To make things worse, my honey's spiritual ego was growing by the minute. He was now the only man in the Israeli Center who had met the Guru and he was having many visions and mystical experiences, many more than all those "old-timers" he met in California. Baba gave him the name Narada. Sage Narada was a great being in ancient India who wrote the famous Bhakti Sutras and was considered to be an authority on all aspects of devotion.

My husband was also experiencing spontaneous writing and was receiving messages through this new and unique ability. He now began to say that he was in fact a re-incarnation of Sage Narada, and used my weak and vulnerable position of being pregnant to take over the leadership of the center. He gave all the lectures "spontaneously," he claimed, and set himself up as "the" spiritual teacher. He quit his job as a music teacher and started charging monthly dues from devotees who came to the center. He also had many of the students come over to do chores.

> *When we don't recognize our inner being, we try to take credit for our past lives, assuming there is such an animal.*
> *We love to think that we were someone important like Cleopatra, Alexander the Greator John the Baptist.*
> *Have you ever heard anyone say that in their past life they were a poor schmuck shining shoes in Buttfuck Lebanon?*

My husband and I lived a very austere and yogic lifestyle, much like in the early years in the ashram. We slept in separate beds and had sex once in a blue moon when he felt it was "appropriate." The sex always left me feeling guilty and depressed. It enhanced my body consciousness, which I was led to believe was taboo, and reminded me that I failed to become a monk.

At times my husband would wake me up in the middle of the night and demand that I leave the bedroom and sleep on the back porch with the howling stray cats so that my vibration wouldn't pollute the highly charged, transcendent and divine encounter that was being bestowed upon him.

To pacify me for having to drag my pregnant body out in the middle of the night, he would tell me that he received messages that our son-to-be was a direct gift from Baba's Guru and would be a great teacher as well. Needless to say, when I delivered a girl it came as quite a blow to his prophetic ego. He refused to believe this and called the hospital saying, "This must be a mistake, check again." Did he really think that doctors and nurses couldn't tell the difference between a boy and a girl?

The Not So "True-Man" Show Meets Goodwill Busting

I knew this Guru trip was wrong and even wrote a letter to Baba about it, but I never got a response. When my daughter was 6 months old, the three of us went to India, taking with us 25 devotees. When we got there, all hell broke loose. Baba found out about my husband's "guru trip" and was livid. Oh, the spiritual politics, when will they ever end.

Needless to say, our 6-month stay there turned into an emotional drama, filled with agony and humiliation. We were continuously called into meetings to discuss all the wrong ways we had handled things at the center and, of course, my husband always seemed to be "under the weather" when these gatherings took place, so I had to get busted on his behalf.

To make things worse, my daughter was terrified of Baba and would have nothing to do with him. My dream of having this child grow up with Baba was starting to crumble. Where did I get the idea that I could have any designs on her life, or anyone's for that matter, anyway? So many parents wish their children would be a certain way and here I was doing the same, only it was "spiritual," so that made it ok. Or did it?!

Well, we returned to Israel with our tails between our legs, and for a short period the egos were laying low. We re-opened the center the "proper" way this time, but within 2 years we encountered tremendous opposition from a group of religious Jews. They threatened to burn our center down. Meditation and yoga were very new in Israel at that time and were considered strange and alien. Baba recommended that we move to Canada and open a center there. We picked Vancouver, BC, since there seemed to be more spiritual activity there at that time, and we re-opened our center in that beautiful part of Canada.

Sleepless Near Seattle

Belonging to Baba's organization allowed us to make quick and solid connections and friendships in Vancouver, but moving to this Canadian city from Israel was an enormous challenge. My husband was a former musician and a wannabe-guru and to make things worse, he knew very few words in English. I used to clean homes for a living in Israel but in Canada, where just about every home is carpeted from wall to wall, my back could not handle all the vacuuming. It was a very tough beginning and we were practically out of money. Fortunately, a devotee found a clerical job for me at his firm and my husband enrolled in a government subsidized English course.

After two years Baba sent one of his swamis to Vancouver, and with the swami's guidance our center became the Vancouver ashram. All the while, I was still bound by my spiritual concepts of being held back by being a wife, a mother and now, an employee in some worldly corporation.

My husband recognized that this was torturing me and offered to take full care of our daughter so that I could be free to become a monk as I always wanted, but I could not do that. I was torn inside. I loved my daughter more than life itself, yet my fabricated sense of separation caused me to strive for the false freedom of stepping out of anything that my belief system considered to be "unspiritual." It took me about eight years to surrender to being a householder or, rather, to be willing to put up with it. It didn't help much that I hated my job. Nothing outside of the ashram interested me!

One night, while the entire Hindu population was celebrating Shivaratri, the night of Shiva that is considered to have the power to grant any wish to those who stay up and chant, and while my husband and daughter were asleep in the tiny room that we shared in the ashram, I sat before our alter and chanted all night with the intent to be able to quit my job and work full-time in the Vancouver ashram.

I didn't know how I was going to make it into work the next morning, since I did not get a moment of sleep. But lo and behold, as I was sluggishly and reluctantly getting ready for the day, my boss called to tell me that because the work load was so low and since I had been sick quite a bit throughout the winter, I could take six months off with pay. After that, I could take more time off and apply for recovery insurance. Bottom line, my wish was fulfilled. From that day on, I became the ashram cook and assistant manager. How wonderful; God heard my prayer and granted my desire.

I was now getting up at 4 a.m. and cooking for the 18 people who lived in the ashram. On weekends we held intensives, so I cooked for 80. At times I gave talks and helped with other organizational aspects of the rapidly growing ashram. I was in my element, feeling good about all the wonderful work I was doing while being completely distracted from my original intent of finding God.

From So-Called Stable To The Grave

Once again, the pendulum swung as it always does and my joy was short lived. On October 2, 1982, as I was stirring the soup for the dinner I was preparing, our swami approached me and gave me the worst news ever. Baba passed away that morning! Everyone had known about this for several hours but had been instructed to keep it from me until I finished cooking. They suspected that I would collapse upon receiving this tragic message, and in fact I did.

Early that morning, just before waking up, I had a dream about Baba. He appeared to me as real as ever and intimated that I may ask him for anything I wanted and it would be granted. The only wish I could think of was that I wanted to serve him and do his work, and as these words came out of my mouth I merged into his being.

Now my whole world was disintegrating within and without. There are no words to describe the devastation. My Guru had left before bestowing self-realization upon me. How could this have happened? Where had I gone wrong? What more could I have done to secure his favour? How else could I have been closer to him while he was alive? And as if all this confusion was not enough, I was now hearing stories, unfortunately from reliable sources, that while I was guilt ridden every time I slept with my "spouse," Baba was having sex with 16-year-old girls in the ashram. Of course, he was a great yogi and was able to pull his semen up instead of ejaculating, but what the fuck!

As my mind went berserk with these endless yet useless doubts and self-examination, something inside me became more peaceful. I spent hours in conversations with the swami, who read to me from Nisargatta's book, I Am

That. I loved what I heard but my loyalty to my deceased Guru drove me to try and connect with his successors.

First I went back to India and desperately attempted to establish a similar relationship with the new Gurus as I had with Baba. Nope, it was just not the same. Prior to his passing, Baba had inaugurated the older daughter and older son of the family that I visited back in the early 70s. There was a huge televised fire ceremony with every high-positioned Indian priest in attendance where Baba announced that he was "giving his power and knowledge" to his two successors. I wasn't there but the video was shown all over the world in every center and ashram that represented Baba's organization.

Today, this all seems so ridiculous to me. How can anyone "inherit" the Kingdom that has always been inside? Is Self-Realisation not an inner gift of one's own Self? If it was possible to give the power and knowledge to another, why wasn't it given to all of us? What were we, chopped liver?

I had met the female successor, who was now called Gurumayi, when she was still in high school. We used to sew together and talk about Baba. Her brother, who was now named Nityananda after Baba's Guru, was five years younger and, as a child, was often chased around the ashram and beaten with a stick for his mischievous behavior. How could they replace my Baba?

> *"A ceremony or an initiation that*
> *does not lead into present moment awareness,*
> *is nothing but a hindrance,*
> *no matter how extravagant, colourful or significant*
> *it may seem to the mind!" – Gabor*

Being back in India helped a bit, since the ashram was still filled with Baba's presence, and I was given the job of managing a huge bookstore that served thousands of devotees. This task took all my attention, most days from 3 a.m. until late in the evening so once again, I was distracted from my original aspiration by excessive "doing."

From The Heat Of India To The Frying Pan of USA In A New York Minute

Immediately after the assassination of Indira Ghandi, all the Westerners had to leave India. I was sent to the U.S. headquarters, the ashram in South Fallsburg in upstate New York, where I spent the next four years. It was a renovated hotel in the beautiful and serene Catskill Mountains. Shortly after arriving there, the political scene with the two successors came to a critical point, which resulted in a split of Baba's kingdom and its sovereigns. Suddenly there was nothing but tremendous turmoil and confusion amongst all.

One night, in sheer anguish, I became lost in deep meditation and found myself crawling into Baba's grave, begging him to help me sort all this shit out. I heard him saying to me, "The only thing you can trust is your own experience." I wasn't 100% sure what that meant, since my many years of outer worship did not offer much introspection, but I noticed that I was slowly beginning to remove myself mentally and psychically from the affairs of the ashram and the morphogenetic field that it engendered.

I had no understanding about what was happening to me. All I knew was that my body was deteriorating and often felt like it was shutting down. I was also suffering immense depression. I wanted so badly to find my own experience and to be the divine self I heard so much about. Yes, little did I realize that unless and until one actually goes inside and *knows* by his/her own experience, which is essentially a being-ness rather than an experience, all else is nothing but "hearsay."

I used to walk for hours in the forests that surrounded the ashram, crying and praying for some kind of deliverance. I did not know how to go within and I had nothing on the outside that even closely resembled the God that I have grown accustomed to worshiping. I was burning inside with questions and doubts. My body was so ill and weak that I could no longer work very much in the ashram.

I had very little desire to live and deep inside, I did not really want to get well. I somehow felt that if I got my health back I would no longer be able to detach myself from the ashram's dramas along with the conceptual spiritual vortex that I had adopted over the years. Instead, I would have to get re-involved in the life and in the environment that were no longer conducive to my inner yearning but rather suffocating my soul.

In a moment of deep desperation, I was prepared to turn to Gurumayi for help and I asked to see her privately. The day finally came and I found myself kneeling before her as my last resort. I began to tell her about my depression; however, before I could complete all I had wished to express,

Gurumayi blurted out, "That's why I keep dogs around me, they have no intellect." She then motioned that the conversation was over. I left the room in greater pain than when I had gone in now that all hope was blown to the wind.

"What the hell did she mean?" I questioned. "How is that helpful to me? What am I supposed to do with my intellect?" Gurumayi's so-called "coaching" was neither comforting nor enlightening. But what else could I expect from someone who just *inherited* her position as a guru?

Shortly after that, Gurumayi sent my family and I back to Canada. This was another very difficult blow since ashram life became my way of living and what I thought was my support. At first I tried to find an alternative. "Perhaps we could move to a small town in upstate New York, somewhere near the ashram," I said to my husband, as I couldn't bear to be so far. I invested so much time and prayer into being able to live a "spiritual life" in a "spiritual place." However, all my attempts to find a closer location, with a possibility of finding work as non-Americans, failed. Finally, a devotee we knew offered a room in her home, which was very near to the ashram. "Perfect solution!" I thought. Or was it?

Naturally, I went up to convey the good news to Gurumayi at darshan time. This was the time at the end of Gurumayi's evening program when everyone lined up to approach her and bow down before her. Some would offer a gift while others were more inclined to ask a question, and she would brush their heads with a long bushy peacock-feather-wand which was scented with aromatic Indian oils.

It was the middle of the summer so there were thousands of people lined up in four rows in a huge outdoor pavilion, where she sat on her throne. Since it took so long for everyone to get through the line, some chose to eat dinner first and line up later while those who had already been through the line went for their supper.

So there were thousands of devotees standing in a long queue in the pavilion and thousands sitting in a gigantic dining room watching the scene around Gurumayi on a huge TV screen. It was finally my turn to go up. I was so sure that Gurumayi would be extremely happy with my solution to remain so close. I worked it all out.

But, shock of all shocks, as soon as I uttered a few words about my brilliant plan she turned to me and, with glaring eyes and a severe tone, proclaimed before everyone present in the pavilion and on the dining room TV screen, "You don't want to listen to me. You just want to do whatever you want to do. So go ahead and do what you want."

Holy shit, thousands of people saw and heard that, the words that vehemently and blatantly declared that I was a disobedient, defiant, headstrong and willful disciple who had no regard for the Guru's instructions. To say that I was crushed, mortified, ashamed and utterly humiliated would be the understatement of all understatements. If there were a creature in existence that was smaller than a single-celled organism it would have been me at that moment. I was dying inside.

Oddly enough, or perhaps because of that, at the same time a strange kind of peace was starting to well up within me. It felt like a premonition, a sense of expectancy for a promising yet unknown future. We humans have been entrained to feel very uncomfortable with not knowing what will happen next. No wonder there are so many successful psychics and fortune tellers. However, this feeling that was growing inside me was not unpleasant. Perhaps the shock of being creamed in front of all those people temporarily stopped my mind and not knowing what the future holds allowed consciousness to come forth, but more on that later. It was comforting, exciting and just as real as the disgrace I had just encountered. Within two weeks, off we went to Toronto, Canada.

> *If Mohammed doesn't*
> *come to the lesson, then*
> *the lesson has to come*
> *to Mohammed!*

Chapter Three

SECOND MISDIRECT - IN RETROSPECT, IT WAS INTELLECT

The Last Straw Or Last Hurrah?

The first few months after leaving the ashram were very difficult. Talk about a culture shock; Toronto is like Vancouver on steroids. It is a huge, very fast-paced and merciless metropolitan city. After so many years in the ashram, I no longer knew how to live a normal family life in the world and had no special vocation to speak of. I never even heard of a resume or a CV.

Once again we were penniless. As you now know, it wasn't the first time that I was broke but this time it really bother me; my daughter was growing rapidly and my health was pretty bad. My husband never really learned how to hold a steady and decent job and so I struggled with a few days here and there doing temp work. There was no one to turn to. I finally wrote to Gurumayi, in an attempt to get some guidance, only to receive the following message, "Sell your stocks of hard times!"

I don't know if this was the last straw or the last hurrah, but from this point on I could not bring myself to visit the meditation center in Toronto and I could no longer chant in the morning as I had done for the past 16 years, regardless of where I lived. My past just simply dropped dead with everything that went with it; no more alter, no pictures of Gurus, no satsangs, no anything, for that matter, that resembled my former life. It was the first time since meeting Baba that I had no instruction, no service role, no mission to fulfil that had to do with his teachings.

Your Shit Is My Bread And Butter

One day my husband went to get a colonic and, being overwhelmed with the amount of money he was charged, came home suggesting that I take a course in colon irrigation. He was hoping that this would generate a better income for us. We did not have enough money for the course, but the owner of the clinic agreed to enroll me for half the fee on the condition that I work for him after I graduate and that I allow him to deduct the rest of my tuition from my salary.

Finally a ray of sunshine, even though my new profession had to do with the place where the sun *don't* shine. I took the course and became a colon therapist. I can't say it was a dream job but there was satisfaction in helping people feel better and, of course, it made for wonderful dinner conversations and filthy jokes.

Fateful Distraction

One of the participants in the course caught my attention. There was a quality about him of a person with a higher purpose in life. When I asked him what he did for a living, he said it would take 17 pages to describe his occupation. He seemed very secretive and reserved, but when I told him that I had been on a spiritual path for 16 years and mentioned Swami Muktananda's name, his demeanor changed and he opened up to me. He told me that he worked for an older gentleman who lectured on metaphysics. His name was Mr. Mills and after he was awarded an Honorary Doctorate of Humanities he was called Dr. Mills.

I had no idea what metaphysics was, but something intrigued me about this. Once I started working there, I met quite a few of this teacher's students who came one by one to get colonics as part of a cleansing program that was recommended to them. This was wonderful; I was having deep and interesting conversations with these people and I met them all from the "bottom" up.

I learned that Dr. Mills spoke spontaneously. He was an author and a poet and the conductor of a group of 10 to 12 singers who performed all over Europe and several times in Carnegie Hall. They called him a renaissance man. I was surprised, though, that not one of the students of Dr. Mills ever tried to convert me or even invite me to one of his lectures. I wanted to meet this man but was told that he only sees people who ask to hear him speak.

I found this very strange since my background was one of running a center that was open to anyone and everyone, and here was this aura of privacy and exclusivity around this man and his teachings. In fact, no one ever talked to me about the actual teachings of Dr. Mills or even mentioned anything that he said.

All they said was that they attended his lectures, usually on Sundays, and then had to go to group classes on Thursdays to re-hear the speech from the weekend. I also found out that anyone who wished to be present at a speaking engagement had to commit to showing up for a minimum of three lectures, as well as the re-hearing classes. After that they would have to either make a lifelong commitment to go to every single event from that point on and pay the full dues, or not come at all.

Dr. Mills' speaking engagements were called *Unfoldments*, and he had this word copyrighted. All participants had to sign a confidentiality agreement prior to their first Unfoldment and they were not allowed to reveal anything that was said. In hindsight, this should have been my cue to stay the hell away from this organization. If his message was one that promoted everyone's birthright to find true freedom, why would it be confidential?

> *Knowing one's true being is everyone's birthright.*
> *The definition of birthright: A right, possession,*
> *or privilege that is one's due by birth.*
> *A birthright is not confidential. It is not a secret,*
> *nor is it the monopoly of a select few.*

Of course, there was an explanation for everything, even this; the words of Dr. Mills had to be confidential so that they wouldn't be misconstrued or taken out of context. Every word had to be just right. Again, in retrospect, here was another clue. The teaching was word-centric, which means it was inherently "content" and not "context." I will get back to that pitfall later.

Guess Who's Coming To Get Rid Of Dinner?

One day I heard that Dr. Mills was scheduled to come to the clinic late in the evening to get a colonic by the owner himself. I also learned that people I treated had been talking to him about me. I wanted very much to meet him so that day, instead of leaving at my usual time of 5 p.m., I stayed on and proceeded to engage in "made-up" odd chores in the hopes that I would somehow bump into this mysterious man. I was in another room when Dr. Mills arrived and missed him when he vanished into the colonic room. No problem, I just continued to futz around looking busy, all the while keeping an alert eye on the door of the colonic room where Dr. Mills was getting his colon irrigated.

Well, he finally came out. He was completely naked, with just a towel around his waist, and was headed to the washroom. When he noticed me standing by he smiled and, with his booming tone, said, "You must be Nurit. I heard you were from Israel."

There was something very familiar about his voice, and seeing the reverence towards him by the few people around I felt honored to have met him. How interesting. My first Guru came to my attention by finding his books in the washroom and here I am meeting my second teacher on his way to the washroom. Hmmm, symbolic much?

As he was leaving the clinic, Dr. Mills invited me to come to his home to hear his singers. I was over the moon. I later found out that he said to some of his followers that I was spiritually advanced. Wow, there we go again. I didn't sleep all night. From rock bottom and an utterly deflated ego, I was now soaring again with spiritual pride.

Miraculously my energy came back and I was healed. Or was I? The universe had created an empty space for me, a void of humility and unfamiliar territory, through degradation, defeat and failure, so that I could find my way back to my original "no-thingness." But once again I managed to fill this gap up and, like everyone else, I fell hook, line and sinker for success and recognition, spiritual success, of course!

The Sound Of Music Meets Keeping Up Appearances

The singers sang beautifully and their voices were exquisite, very loud and without the use of microphones. There were sounds that I have never heard before. The event took place in what Dr. Mills called his music room, the largest room in his home, which could seat at least 80 people. It was packed with smiling people, all dressed up very elegantly and all focused on Dr. Mills, waiting for an opportunity to shake his hand and tell him how wonderful the music was.

Dr. Mills played the role of conductor and host. He wore the most extravagant suit I have ever seen in my life and was decked out to the nines with a huge gold necklace covered with precious stones, a gold and diamond studded watch, an enormous bracelet befitting a king and several rings, the sizes and weights of which could tip someone over if they were not evenly balanced on both hands.

Dr. Mills' entire house was like a museum, with pictures and objet d'art everywhere and the most lavish chandeliers hanging from just about every ceiling. There were several very fancy and spacious living rooms, two elegant dining rooms with elaborate tables and chairs that could seat at least 18 people, a huge library, six to eight bedrooms each with its own bathroom, a few other marbled and gold leafed guest washrooms, two enormous and majestic foyers, and that was just on the first floor.

The upper level had a king size lavish apartment on one side, which was Dr. Mills' private quarters, and a queen-size apartment on the other side where his sister stayed when she visited. I heard that Dr. Mills' living area included a separate walk-in closet just for his hundreds of designer shoes.

The lower level had an indoor swimming pool, a gym, another humongous library with transcriptions of the thousands of hours of lectures that Dr. Mills delivered over the years, a few more bedrooms and bathrooms, and a sauna. The property was very beautifully landscaped with a koi fish pond, a tennis court, and several patios; I think you get the picture.

I later found out that Dr. Mills had a few other properties as well, including an inn in northern Ontario where he held summer retreats. After a while he sold this estate because his students weren't working hard enough to maintain it. Of course, he then purchased some other properties in the Turks and Caicos and in Quebec, but I digress.

The important thing was that he maintained this excessively extravagant life style, as he said, to be an example for his students and to demonstrate to them what is possible to achieve. Mind you, not one of his followers ever had the means to live the same way or even close to it. How could they? So much of their income went to support Dr. Mills. There were monthly dues of over $400, plus his disciples were expected to give 10% of their gross income, yes, before taxes, as a tithe to Dr. Mills. After all, he gave up his "not as profitable" career as a piano teacher in order to devote all his time to his spiritual students, with the exception of the few private businesses he still held on to for quite some time.

Of course, it was stated that money should not keep a person away, meaning if one didn't have enough money to pay the full dues one could pay less for a while. However, it was also implied that if you "practised" the teachings you would be able to manifest enough income to afford the fees. There was never a shortage of spiritual peer pressure.

> *Presence speaks for itself, especially in silence and simplicity. An awakened teacher does not give a flying fuck about keeping up appearances.*

Another explanation Dr. Mills often offered was that, in a sense, he acted as the redeemer of St. Francis of Assisi. He was establishing the fact that one can be an enlightened mystic, a man of God, and still be wealthy at the same time. But what can I say? Baba had quite a kingdom too, so the wealth around Dr. Mills didn't bother me much. To me, the fact that he was from the west, living in the world and running his own businesses, served at that time as an example of "Being in the world, but not of it" which, up until this point, I had only heard about out of the mouths of monks who lived in ashrams.

My husband, on the other hand, did not share my view of Dr. Mills. While I saw a most accomplished man who was larger than life exuding the kind of creativity that could only have come from a divine source, the spiritual concepts which my husband nurtured did not include a teacher from the west, let alone a business man. So you can imagine how he felt when I announced that I was headed to Dr. Mills' inn in Northern Ontario to attend an Unfoldment. He threatened to leave me if I went but Baba's words from within his grave, "You have to go by your own experience" suddenly came in handy and I went anyway.

The 180 Degree Change: From Sloppy Surrender To Intellectual Contender

I can't say that I understood much of what Dr. Mills said in the Unfoldment. However, he spoke spontaneously in a Shakespearian type of highly advanced English, interspersed with poetry that just flowed out of him with great ease. For some reason that impressed the hell out of me, or should I say my mind was extremely awestruck. For the first time in its existence, it was confronted by divine ideas that it could not fathom and it was experiencing a verbal expression of that, which was considered to be beyond articulation.

"Anyone who can speak like this must be enlightened," I thought. "This must be the real deal. What I have learned before was most likely a lower level, since I understood it perfectly. This is different and subtle, therefore it is more in keeping with the higher Self." Or, as I would *now* say, "More in keeping with my conceptual notion of the *Higher Self*, along with all the reference points I had acquired over my years of spiritual sophistry."

There was quite a bit of guilt inside me for leaving my previous path and joining this new group, but I believed that my loyalties must always be to the supreme Self and this, I felt, could lead me closer to my original goal. I was now happy again as I had new hope. Little did I realize that hope was all I ever lived on and how deceiving it was.

When I got home, seeing how happy I was due to my new discovery, my husband changed his mind about leaving me and decided to go to the lectures with me. We began to attend every Unfoldment. We also participated in all the mandatory re-hearing classes, which meant listening in a group to the previous lecture that Dr. Mills gave and discussing the ideas.

We were committed to studying the transcripts of the lectures which were given after each session. This included looking up just about every other word in a regular king-size dictionary as well as the Indo-European root dictionary to ensure that we analyzed the hell out each sentence with our puny intellects. Ironically, we were frequently scolded for being too intellectual.

We also took the oath that every student was expected to take. This was a ceremony where one swears allegiance and unwavering fidelity to the Self by pledging full commitment to support the representative of that said "Self," namely, Dr. Mills. Or, in layman's terms, never missing a class unless you are on your death bed, and paying the monthly dues.

> *So let me get this straight. I have to*
> *take an oath, so that I can remain loyal*
> *to what I already am? You mean, to my very own essence?*
> *You mean, to that from*
> *which I can never be separated even if I try?*
> *Hmmmmm.*

New Broom, Clean Mind

There was one other extremely important component that played a huge part in my enchantment with Dr. Mills and his world. It is so subtle that I only just recently became aware of it. It is the element of "newness" itself.

Suddenly everything was new for me. From the simplicity of ashram life I found myself surrounded by elegance; most of the ideas and concepts in the lectures I had never heard before; mystical experiences and devotion were outdated and the intellect took center stage; the use of the language was different; the boring repetitive Sanskrit mantras were replaced by complex long sentences that, at times, made up an entire paragraph; chanting rituals and holy ceremonies gave way to art and fashion shows, and to concerts with unheard of sounds and notes; meat came back and garlic and onions were out. Everything was brand spanking new.

A common yet amazing phenomenon occurs when the mind is exposed to a fresh and unfamiliar experience. When it loses its ability to locate and to latch on to any of its hosts of reference points, its habitual functions of comparing, equating, relating, measuring against, matching, linking, associating, contrasting, evaluating, and creating a narrative, all these are briefly neutralized. The poor bugger we so adoringly call "our mind" can finally catch a break. Its busyness subsides for a while and in those still moments consciousness makes a brief entrance. Thus, we are able to temporarily relax into presence. This is why "not knowing" is more powerful than "knowing."

By the way, I am not talking here about presence of mind or the presence of a charismatic personality. Presence is like gravity; as soon as there is no mental reference point and nothing is shoving it up into the attic, it defaults back into its original position of Oneness, or of the nothingness of silent space. Unfortunately, in most cases, we don't realize the inner emergence of presence and we pass on the holy credit to the external cause which dazzled our mind and gave it a pause.

This is why people love to travel so much. The mind is engulfed with newness and shuts up for a while. This also lends an entirely different explanation to why our re-hearing classes faded in comparison to the live Unfoldments. Dr. Mills had the rare gift of being able to articulate ideas in ever new ways. No Unfoldment was like another. But when we listened to the recordings of Unfoldments that we already heard, our minds no longer considered the words to be fresh. It was a RE-hearing, and we were RE-engaging ourselves over again with the same material and with all kinds of reference points, opinions and word research.

> *"A poor person's 'moment with no reference point' is the same as a rich person's 'moment with no reference point.' Whether you make your first billion dollars, or get your first washing machine, the momentary cessation of the mind's activities is the same. The measure of stillness, when the mind has temporarily stopped, is not proportionate to the size of the object or event, that brought about the newness." – Gabor*

The Resurrection Of Sage Narada

After three years, my husband had his fill of this teaching and decided it was time to move back to Israel. I refused to leave Canada and my new teacher and this seemed like a great opportunity to free myself from the marriage that I had been wanting to get away from for the past 17 years. So off he went on his own.

At first he opened a colonic clinic and then he set himself up as a Guru. Using what he learned from Baba and from Dr. Mills, he created his own style of teaching. He officially changed his name to Sage Narada and there were lots of lost souls who followed him and paid him with their time and hard earned money to become initiated by the great reincarnated Sage and to receive prophetic promises of a future based on spiritual and psychic experiences. And, of course, getting colonics on a regular basis was also a requirement that his disciples had to meet.

I spoke with my ex-husband only once after he left. He told me all about his visions and other spiritual experiences that led him to realize that he was the reincarnation of this great sage and that he was, indeed, self-realized. Most of what he described sounded very much like what Baba had narrated in his book *The Play of Consciousness*. I wasn't the least bit impressed since, by then, I already knew that all these were nothing but psychic sign posts. And besides, why would anyone want to be a reincarnation of anyone? Is the present incarnation so meaningless?

I definitely could not take his "final confirmation" too seriously. He told me that one morning, as he was getting out of bed, he noticed a ring of mouse shit that had been formed all around his bed. Since the mouse was considered in the Hindu tradition to be the vehicle of the elephant god, Lord Ganesh, this must have been a sign that he had "arrived." I don't think my ex-husband will ever live that one down. Oye vey, poor little mouse, talk about spiritual pressure! No wonder it crapped itself. Or was that mouse in need of a colonic?

But all kidding aside, God bless the man. He finally got what he wanted. Today I see even more clearly how deceiving those experiences can be. I have come to perceive that the "real" is actually not at all an "experience" any more than it is a "state of mind." And it most certainly cannot be described in words. In fact, any attempt to apply words can only invalidate it. But more on that later. For now let me continue to narrate my own mind's delusions and how far it has taken me.

Getting Lost In Mind-Based Intellectual Orgies

Basically, I spent 15 years believing I had finally found the real path to God. I went to every lecture, each re-hearing class, and all rehearsals and performances of Dr. Mills' singers in Canada or the U.S. I attended every workshop and retreat and had a seat on the board of directors for a while. I cleaned his home and worked in his garden on the weekends and even got a job at one of Dr. Mills' companies, which I loathed, just so that I could have every opportunity to see him or hear him speak.

Occasionally, I was invited for dinner at his home, and at other times I would request to see him after his dinner parties when he would allow some people to join in for coffee. By the way, his dinner parties were extremely lavish, elegant and formal. They took place in one of his fancy dining rooms where there was a huge oval custom-made and beautifully set table with 18 to 20 gorgeous velvety chairs around it. There were kitchen staff preparing the meals and waiters dressed in starched uniforms who served the gourmet food in silence and precision.

Dr. Mills and his dinner guests ate and drank out of very expensive china and crystal, using ornate sterling silver or gold plated cutlery which Dr. Mills purchased from specialty stores all over the world. He never missed an opportunity to tell everyone at his table where he got these precious items and how costly they were. Anyone who broke anything, whether they were guests, servers, or kitchen staff, would be expected to pay for their replacement, even though they were nearly impossible to replace.

Also, there were so many rules about how to eat at his table, I actually had to take a crash course in proper dining etiquette before I was invited to dinner. How about that for a big change? Not exactly the same as sitting on the floor and eating with my hands off a grape-leaf plate in India, huh?

I spent hours by the phone, waiting in anticipation for any call from Dr. Mills' house inviting me to come. I had no life of my own. My mood, my attitude, my disposition, my state of mind, all these were predicated upon my direct contact with Dr. Mills, or the absence of it. If I was summoned and got to see him, my ego felt special and elated; if I missed an opportunity to be with him, the ego was dejected and deflated.

My values, my likes and dislikes, my judgements, my preferences, my taste in food, music, attire, jewelry, and hair style, were all based on his. He didn't like women wearing pants, so I always wore a skirt or a dress. If you wore jeans, you might as well have had the "Antichrist" symbol tattooed on your forehead.

Dr. Mills did not permit us to eat garlic or raw onions. He read us an article by a doctor who concluded that a group of people attending a conference were sleepy after lunch, since the Indian food that they ate contained garlic. Really? Ya-don't-think it had anything to do with the deep-fried, heavily greased and excessively sweetened dishes and desserts that Indian food is so famous for? I still can't believe I bought that and stopped eating garlic, one of the healthiest foods on this planet. Mind you, I recently found out that, on occasion, Dr. Mills relished pasta sauce that was full of garlic. Apparently he just didn't like smelling it on us.

Once again, I gave myself totally; every moment and every cent were dedicated to my new path. I was now intensely studying, morning, noon and evening, these splendid, outstanding and most impressive metaphysical teachings which no one really "got!" Yes, it was actually confirmed to me by Dr. Mills himself that we never "got" it. I researched the root meanings of words and memorized whole pages but, once again, it was all "about" and never "how to." It was always about what "his" (Dr. Mills') experience was, what the meaning of soul was according to "his" understanding, what the Truth, Self, Reality, Source, etc. was by "his" very eloquent definitions but without the aliveness of the innate presence of the participants' innermost origin. Here too my learning was based on "hearsay!"

I could never see it at that time since the mind can't see itself, but the entire teachings and every bit of that path took place in the mind and by a mind. After the 16 years of sloppy and spacy Bhakti (devotion), my intellect was delighted with all the new knowledge and became highly skilled at analyzing, conceptualizing, categorizing, verbalizing, elucidating, explicating, articulating; I could go on.

I wrote a book and several plays and did live story-telling in theatres, reciting and quoting Dr. Mills' poetry and prose. We all got high on his words. Every now and then he would correct someone for using the wrong word in expressing a "divine" idea which, by the way, is also a mind exercise, and the person's jaw would drop in reverence and awe and they would let out a sigh of utter amazement. Bottom line, we were all having intellectual orgasms. How satisfied I was. And who wants to wake up from such a pleasant dream?

Dr. Mills spoon-fed us information and content which made us dependent on him. It always bothered me that I had to rely on a teacher, or on someone I believe "had IT," in order to experience some sort of peaceful state. I remember thinking how fortunate Dr. Mills was to be with himself, whereas I had to wait by the phone for an opportunity to spend a few hours with him and hope that the bliss would last a bit longer. I asked him one day, "Sometimes, especially when I hear you speak, I am in a really good state. How can I sustain it so that it doesn't just come and go?"

"You can't sustain it, dear." He replied. *"IT is what sustains you."*

"Great reply," I thought. And yes, it was a very smart answer for keeping me in the intellect, as most mental "Aha" moments do. But little did I realize at that time how un-useful it was, as it was not a "Heart Aha." I now know that this answer was faulty at its core. I had asked about a state of mind, induced by tantalizing intellectual stimulants. By its very nature it comes and goes. There is nothing steady or secure about any "state of mind." His answer would have been accurate if he had referred to Presence as what "sustains me."

However, even then, by merely saying that, the door to freedom would still not open. How could I access it with just words? Unless he could demonstrate the "how to" and guide me into the Presence within me, which is the only stable and lasting existence anyone can have, and actually does have but is not aware of it, there could be no resolution or answer to my question.

> *Offering a clever answer that*
> *satisfies the questioning mind*
> *is like giving a shot of whiskey*
> *to an alcoholic in denial.*

Dr. Mills had great statements that were 100% accurate from the mind's perspective, but without being present, and without a silent mind, they were useless or even dangerous because as soon as the mind learned these so-called truths one would become immunized to presence. The mind believed it knew and understood THAT, which it cannot fathom. If I may be so bold, accepting these verities and believing they bear a transcendent nature is spiritual suicide.

A Shit Sandwich Is Always A Shit Sandwich

Dr. Mills talked about "Riding the horse of the mind" or "It doesn't take time to think right" or "Behave as if you were already THAT." All these are great and smart but the mind can't ride the horse of the mind. Remember Billy, the goat? That would be like asking him to guard the cabbage. Thinking right puts it in the realm of right and wrong, if one understands this with the mind. And behaving "as if" is cultivated behaviour which never lasts. When one is present, there is nothing to cultivate. All the appropriate attitudes and conducts occur on their own.

Changing thoughts from negative to positive and putting on a "happy face" as we were often expected to do, God forbid there would be a bad mood, keep one very busy in the mind. Any change done with the mind never lasts. The mind lives in duality. Although it may be a 180 degree change it will soon swing back. It is like moving filth around in a pigpen without ever actually **re**moving it. What is required is a 90 degree shift by transcending the mind altogether.

One of the exercises we were instructed to do was called "The Test of Reality." You basically write down on a piece of paper everything about yourself that is mortal or changing, your opinions, your form, your thoughts, the environment, associates, careers, friends, family, beliefs, etc. etc., until you reach a point where there is nothing you can add. At that point, Dr. Mills said, "Everything on the piece of paper is you and everything that isn't is the Creative Principle," a synonym he used for God.

"Brilliant," says the mind. "Now I know what the Self or God is." Yes, the mind thinks it does but the Soul does not and neither does the heart. It is a great concept and several others have used it in their own way; however, it is nothing but a mental practice with the use of clever words.

Dr. Mills put a lot of emphasis on words and wanted us to practise using them in a unique way. We were to use the word "I" only when referring to the Higher Self, God, or Consciousness, and the words "you" or "me" when speaking about the little "i" that identifies with the personality. Again, this routine, when done without being present, without actually Being Consciousness, is nothing but mental masturbation. Not only is one shoving under the carpet the personal identity and pretending it is not there, but this very identity is now growing by leaps and bounds by adding intellectual metaphysics to its mix.

> *Piling up intellectual metaphysical*
> *concepts on top of a false identity, is like*
> *attempting to improve the taste of a shit sandwich,*
> *by slopping lots of mayonnaise on it. It would take*
> *more than a Miracle-whip.*

M.O.S.A.D. – The Goggles Of Misguided Acquiescing Devotees

I considered myself very fortunate, since I was quite close to Dr. Mills, and had many occasions to witness how he was behind the scenes when he was not on stage or in front of a camera. I so wanted to, and had to, believe he was the same holy man that I had built up in my mind that I neglected to perceive all the clues that never failed to show up both in subtle and obvious ways.

It is rather embarrassing for me to admit the blatant ones, thus I will only mention a few here for those who still wear the same spiritual rosy glasses that I had on for so many years, and which I now call M.O.S.A.D., "The Goggles of Misguided Acquiescing Devotees." Mosad in Hebrew means "institution," and it is high time to break away from this kind of institution and to start seeing the real picture.

Upon telling Dr. Mills that my Indian teacher used to say, "Do as I say, not as I do," he was rather dismayed to hear this and claimed that he himself was serving as an example for his students. Nonetheless, I remember spending countless hours hearing Dr. Mills bad-mouthing others and singing his own praises about his great accomplishments in the arts and with words, and how no one could ever speak like he did, nor would anyone be able to emulate him even after his passing; the way he healed certain individuals who didn't show adequate appreciation; the financial support he gave to some poor Eastern European people, and invitations he offered others to visit him in Canada.

I can't entirely blame him since, in my gratitude, I did my share of feeding his ego by frequently voicing my admiration of him. I just never expected my expressions of appreciation to go to his head, which I assumed had already been transcended.

Although there were many very ardent feminine devotees around him who served him day and night with tremendous dedication and loyalty, Dr. Mills never missed an opportunity to belittle women in general and to speak of them disparagingly. According to him, if a man ever left his side or departed from his milieu, it was always the fault of a woman and if a lady preferred to live alone instead of sharing accommodations with other students, it was definitely because she intended to have sexual affairs. He painted females as manipulative and conniving creatures, ever on the prowl to hook men, feed off their power, and castrate them.

Hearing these words, I often felt that I had no chance in hell to ever be close to my teacher, let alone be enlightened. Believe it or not, at times I even entertained the idea of getting a sex change. Luckily I was well aware of how terrible I would look without make up so I dropped this idea mighty fast.

Unfortunately, women were not the only victims of his criticism. I had the occasional disadvantage of hearing Dr. Mills speak ill behind the backs of so many of his existing followers, as well as those who chose to leave his association. He would condemn anyone from reeking of garlic to sneaking a glance at a woman; from not sending a thank you card for dinner soon enough to calling him Dr. Mills instead of Dr. Mills after he received this honorary title; for not wanting to move into his home if this was a man whom he liked (hint hint) to being jealous of someone who was living in his home.

I recently watched a YouTube video by Osho in which he said that he did not mind at all if any of his students left him or found another teacher in the event that they felt it would assist in their awakening. I also heard Eckhart Tolle say that his wish was that someday people would no longer buy his books since, in their awakened state, they would have no need for them.

This was extremely refreshing after having heard Dr. Mills say, time and again, in private, of course, that he was concerned with people leaving him since it affected his income. He believed that any student that left his teachings should continue to pay the monthly dues. Clearly, his focus was on his revenue and not on the seekers' spiritual well-being.

The list goes on and on but for now, I feel prompted to express my deep regret for not seeing the ugliness of this behaviour sooner and, more importantly, for allowing myself to be swept up in this game of judgment. I hereby offer my sincere apologies to anyone I have ever criticized in my unconscious state of being a blind follower.

Don't get me wrong. Overall, it was not a negative experience. I became very creative, my English improved tremendously, and having to fork out so much money for lectures and retreats I kept upgrading my professional skills and career. I was certainly getting my worldly shit together and for that I am grateful, but that was not why I was on a path. There are all kinds of great courses out there which are much cheaper that I could have taken for that. My desire to find God never diminished only now, I was blinded to the fact that I was getting further and further away from this objective by using my mind to find THAT which was not only out of its league, but also in an entirely different dimension.

Who Knew?

As I mentioned earlier, during my years with Dr. Mills I had written a book and several plays that were performed at his retreats, all of which were interlaced with quotes from his lectures and books. A few months before he passed away, one of my plays was performed in his large music room with the help of a few fellow students who enacted the various roles. When the show was over and it was time for Dr. Mills to offer his comments, I was astonished to hear him say that I should re-write the entire play without using any of his quotes. He explained that audiences would not be able to grasp the full meaning of his words since they were spoken to a specific crowd at a difference time.

This came as a great shock to me, but what surprised me even more was that no one else out of the 50 or 60 people who watched the performance heard him say that. I had no idea how I was to accomplish this task and if I would even be able to express such lofty ideas in my own words. I realized at that moment how dependent I was on the power of Dr. Mills' eloquence and creative expression, to the point of suppressing my own.

A few month before, I visited Chandra Alexander, a friend I met in India whom I hadn't seen for many years. I kept going on and on about Dr. Mills and all of his accomplishments in an attempt to impress her. However, at one point she stopped me in mid-sentence and said quite powerfully, "Nurit! What did YOU do?" This really startled me as I realized that I couldn't speak of any achievement of mine since most of the words I wrote or recited were not my own. This question was now gnawing at me and I could not for the life of me shake off the effect it had on me.

I went back to the drawing board and began to write a new play. I called it "How Long Is the Now?" and structured it in a way that all the high teachings it was to convey would be spoken by characters who were androgynous and who existed in a realm beyond time. In other words, most of the dialogues in the script had to be enunciated in the present tense and in non-dual terms. Somehow, intuitively I felt that writing this way would help me stay closer to what I imagined my origin to be.

Needless to say, this was a most challenging and painstaking undertaking as I was beginning to see how deeply imbedded "time" is within a language such as English. It seemed so ironic to me how much "time" was required to attempt to express the "timeless." And by the "time" the script was completed, Dr. Mills' "time" on this plane had come to an end after suffering a long and painful illness. He never got to see the finished product.

*"The NOW is an existential status.
It is not a small piece, stolen away
from time."* – Gabor

Chapter Four

ALONE AT LAST, FOR BETTER OR FOR WORSE

Another Guru Bites The Dust

After Dr. Mills passed away, in late 2004, I was extremely surprised to find myself with so many questions and very much a "searcher." The reason this perturbed me is because I was convinced that I had found the absolute teaching and had considered myself to be a "finder" not a "seeker." Once again my teacher died and left me hanging. The pain was excruciating, to say the least. I received the news of his death while still at work. If it wasn't for my daughter and son-in-law who came to get me, I don't know how I would have drove myself home.

By now I had close to 40 years on the spiritual path and, although I knew I did not want to have anything to do with another Guru, I was still going to various courses and seminars and studying all kinds of new age books. I guess it was time to hear my own voice for a change, although I was not at all accustomed to doing that. Heck, I didn't even know what type of music I liked or what kind of clothes I preferred to wear.

My first step was to get away from the group of Dr. Mills' followers. This was very tough since many of them were good friends whom I loved dearly. However, it became very clear to me that I needed to distance myself from "group think." Also, for some reason unknown to me at the time, I could no longer read Dr. Mills' books, listen to his lectures on CD, or hear his music. That chapter in my life was over and it seemed necessary to make a clean break from it.

Of course, this was not easy, as now I not only lost my mentor of 15 years but with his loss all my associates were also gone. I had no other friends and didn't even know how to acquire them since I never needed to. Like it or not, like "them" or not, I was always surrounded by people who were following the same path that I was on. This was the first time in my life that I was completely alone, apart from my daily job and my loving daughter.

How Long Is The Now?

Producing my new play "How Long Is the Now" seemed like a good idea at this stage, no pun intended. It would keep me connected somehow to what I had learned and at the same time it would allow me to explore more deeply my own creativity. In 2005 I submitted the script to a Script of the Year contest, sponsored by the Theatre on Main Street in Newmarket, Ontario. My play won and I was awarded the use of the theatre for six nights at no cost. A friend from work helped me find amateur actors and the work began.

One of my actors in a leading role was an officer with the Toronto Police, and it was his first time on stage. After the first reading of the script he asked me if the play was written based on the teachings of Eckhart Tolle. At that time I hadn't heard of Eckhart yet.

Rehearsals were a lot of fun and the performances were all very successful. The theatre was full each night and some people came more than once to see it. Oddly enough, there were some folks in the audience who had a center for Eckhart Tolle's teachings in their home. They too asked me if the play was inspired by his work.

Wow! I was really intrigued, so I began to read the books and listen to the tapes of Eckhart Tolle. It was astonishing to find so many similarities between his writings and mine. I could see why those people thought the play was connected somehow to Eckhart's teachings. But little did I realize that my understanding of what I read in his books was merely intellectual since I kept comparing his words to those of Dr. Mills. I didn't truly "get it" on a deep level at all, and I can only say that today since now I do.

This, again, is how our spiritual reference points rob us from of own being. When we mentally compare things to what we learned before, the mind gets so busy "doing the path" that a huge bolder is created. The intellect becomes intensely satisfied, thus we go deeper into the slumber of illusion and keep snoring. This is the great danger of using common spiritual phases, even the "non-dualistic" ones like "the now," "presence," "go into your body," etc. We hear these words and immediately say, "Oh, yes, I've heard that before, yeah, yeah, I know that already." Bang! We shot ourselves in the proverbial spiritual foot. It would be wise to notice if your mind is playing that trick on you as you read this book.

And here is an extreme case. A woman once told me that she knew what Reiki was, since she drank Japanese tea. Oh, how desperate the mind is to compare and to draw conclusions. Sorry, Jesus, it may take a while for people to "Be like little children." Heaven may have to wait after all unless, of course, we can finally learn to side step the mind when we are headed, or rather "beheaded," that way.

Who Are You, Mr. MacDreamy?

Very soon after Dr. Mills' final departure, I started having an unusual recurring dream that kept appearing every now and again for about five years. There was no particular story or plot to it, just a man showing up whose face I could not see. This fellow would embrace me and hold me with incomparable warmth, love and silence. Each time this transpired, I became completely and utterly still inside, not a ripple of thought, belief, emotion or even the slightest notion that could resemble an understanding or a description of what was taking place, in what seemed to be an empty space. Even the words used here are inaccurate and inadequate to say the least.

This absolute stillness, this profound presence of nothingness, was unlike anything I had ever witnessed before. I could not even call it an experience, but rather an immersion in a most peaceful thought-free existence.

By this time I had been single and alone for about 13 years and having these periodic dreams began to ignite in me a slight desire to find a partner. I say "slight" since I had been carrying a sizable resistance to being in a relationship. Nonetheless, at the same time I felt quite strongly that I would recognize the man I was to be with by the peace of his embrace and by the intense stillness that his presence would incite within me, just as it was occurring over and over in those dreams. I was also very inspired by three of the actors who performed in my play. Each one of them found the life partner of their dreams at a mature age and were truly exemplary couples. Witnessing this caused me to re-evaluate my previous notions of being in a relationship.

Ok, so now what? After all these years, how would I know how to find a man? I joined a few online dating sites and went to several singles events. I met many men but none were the least bit interesting or even remotely spiritual. Out went the *Eckhart Tolle* books and in came the *Law of Attraction* books and tapes and any material I could find by Abraham Hicks. I spent every free moment learning and practicing how to manifest and co-create what I wanted in life.

A dear friend of mine wanted me to establish a meet-up group for people who were interested in Abraham Hicks. I really didn't want to get involved with any type of congregation nor did I care to organize anything. However, she didn't have a credit card and promised that she would do all the work if I just took care of the initial online registration for this meet-up. I wouldn't even have to attend any of the meetings.

So I did as my friend requested, and I posted the preliminary invitation to the meet-up without any intention of showing up. A few days later I received an email from a man by the name of Gabor Harsanyi. He wrote me a private email saying that he was going to be out of town on the day of the meeting and asked if I would have a coffee with him at another time. My rule was that I would never meet a man without having first seen his picture. However, his name struck a chord with me.

Gabor Harsanyi. Wow, what a strong vibration it had. "Gabor" sounded like the Hebrew word "Gibor," which means brave or heroic. This was a name with very male overtones. Also, I was convinced that "Harsanyi" was a Persian name. What to do? No pictures, but his "vibes" were calling out to me, or was it those good old reference points?! So I agreed to meet him at the Starbucks that was closest to my home, you know, just in case.

Where's My Persian Prince?

I arrived at Starbucks a few minutes early; funny, I remember exactly what I was wearing, and was looking around to find my tall, *dark* and handsome Persian prince. Suddenly a tall, *white* and handsome fellow approached me, not the least bit Persian, and introduced himself as Gabor.

"Oh!" I exclaimed with great surprise. "I thought you were Persian."

"No," he said with a thick accent that I couldn't possibly identify. "I am from Hungary."

Well, our first date was wonderful. My usual awkwardness in speaking with a strange man, after being single for so long, was replaced by the comfortable feeling that this person could be a friend. It was the weekend of the Canadian Thanksgiving and we talked for hours. What was most noticeable and impressive was that Gabor was the best listener I have ever met in my life. Also, he did not even remotely try to impress me. We continued to see each other on the weekends and we spoke on the phone every evening for about a month. Our conversations were amazing. I remember till this day everything we talked about.

The Spiritual Ego – The One-Upmanship's Best Friend

Well, what can I say. After a month my spiritual ego got the better of me and I wasn't able to see who or what was in front of my nose. Or should I say, by cutting off the relationship I actually "cut off my nose to spite my face."

Being with Dr. Mills for so many years, I developed an elitist attitude. Many times I heard Dr. Mills say that after he leaves this world, his students will be sought out. People will be searching for us and admiring us for being the "only ones" who were fortunate enough to have known him. Hmmm, sounds a bit like the chosen people, doesn't it? My mind was too busy showing off all the spiritual knowledge I had acquired and putting Gabor down by finding nothing but faults with him.

"Oh my God, he wears sandals with socks," my mind would critique.

"And that shirt he has on, was that not the same shirt he wore on our last date? Doesn't he have nicer clothes? And why does he take the subway? Doesn't he have a car? How come he lives in Chinatown? What kind of man lives in that godforsaken neighborhood?"

"Oh, and the 'F' bombs he throws around with no regard to my delicate ears. Doesn't he realize the importance of using an appropriate vocabulary? I just spent 15 years analysing the hell out of words and making sure I used them accurately, yet he has no regard for verbal elegance!"

I just could not get his simplicity and he certainly was not impressing me, nor was he trying to. Yeah, about that. "Why isn't he trying to impress me?" I wondered, as most blondes would. "He couldn't really like me that much if he is not attempting to dazzle me like everyone else always has, right?"

Looking back, my criticism of him made no sense but, at that time, this was too much for my pure and highly evolved soul. Yes, I am definitely being sarcastic. Besides, by now it was already 16 years that I had been alone and I wasn't going to give up my comfort zone. Oh, who am I kidding? Something about him scared me. Intuitively, I must have felt that being with him would result in major transformation and my mind, the ruler of my world at that time, would have nothing to do with that.

Which Came First, The Chicken Mind Or The Cosmic Egg?

I was now heavily into co-creating, maintaining a positive attitude, and thinking only good thoughts. Not as easy as it sounds, don't try it at home! I was going more frequently to law of attraction lectures and events and to singles parties. Oddly enough, every now and then Gabor would show up at the same place, somehow.

The first time we bumped into each other, my mind did somersaults when I heard Gabor saying, "Most people are insane." I immediately corrected him by saying, "No, everyone is enlightened, they just don't know it yet." Today I realize that he was actually talking about the insanity of allowing the human mind to be in full control, which has become the norm in most everyone's life. Living in my own head, I was not able to hear him clearly and so I used my mind to find a "positive" response, and a stupid one at that, in order to rectify his statement, which was perfectly accurate to begin with.

At another occasion, Gabor appeared at a singles backyard barbeque that I was at. We started talking and at first it was very nice, like meeting an old friend. After all, he was the only one at the party with whom I could have a meaningful conversation. I was telling him about my attempts at manifesting things as per Abraham Hicks' teachings, and he was talking about presence. This was when I asked him my first and memorable question, "Ok, so you're present, so now what?"

Without intending it to be so, Gabor's response was the most shocking news and a major blow to my ego. "The difference between your spiritual path and what I am about," he said, "is that you are doing it with the mind and I am not." Holy shit, my mind was just hit with a sledge hammer. It has never felt so exposed and it was raging. Little did I realize that this was the first most significant, important and transforming moment in my entire awakening process.

"That's ok," he continued in his peaceful and nonchalant manner, as the rest of the people at the party were stuffing their faces. "We can just agree to disagree."

Today Gabor says that he never even noticed that I was so upset with this remark. To him it was no big deal. He was just stating a fact and it was devoid of any judgement whatsoever.

I was stewing all night! For me, there was nothing nonchalant about this. How could he say that to me? I had been studying with a metaphysician for 15 years. The root meaning of Metaphysics is "*beyond*" the physical world. I have been learning to transcend, haven't I? I have memorized so many statements about transcending the mind or "riding the horse of the mind," as Dr. Mills so eloquently put it. How could I, of all people, be in the mind? Hmmmm, I wonder what it was that was so infuriated? Wanna take a wild guess?

Could it be that the mind is so brilliant and powerful that it can learn, explain, regurgitate, elucidate, explicate, and masticate all kinds of spiritual truths, all the while concealing this manipulative act from us and making us believe that we have actually transcended it? Even though we are so lost in it? Wow, bravo mind! For now you seem to own humanity. No wonder it abhors simplicity and silence.

The next day I was stuck for four hours at the airport, waiting to fly to New Jersey on a business trip. Oh dear, more time to think. You'll never guess what I was thinking about, or should I say, mulling over, and over, and over. So I found a free computer and wrote an email to Gabor saying, "Ok. Let's agree to disagree, and when I get back from my trip, perhaps we could meet and talk further."

So we met one more time and ironically enough, we went to see a movie called "The Love Guru." But even though we tried to hook up again, I kept finding something wrong with him in spite of the fact that he was unlike anyone I had ever met. Gabor was the only man who never tried to impose his values on me. He always showed interest in me without ever making me feel judged and again, I just couldn't get over what an exceptional listener he was. I could tell him anything and he was right there with every word I uttered. Till this day, I can't believe I allowed myself to overlook these unusual qualities only to focus on what my mind found as flaws. By the way, did I mention that he was an excellent listener? Just checking.

And so ignoring these unexpected encounters with Gabor, I kept meeting other men, only to find each one more shallow and disappointing than the next. I had a coach who helped me define my relationship goals and I made a list of all the qualities and traits I was looking for in a man. I kept finding new and improved manifestation seminars that taught the latest and greatest techniques.

I even took an extensive life coaching course where the participants coached the bejesus out of me. The best recommendation at that time came from Spiritual Mentor and Relationship Coach, Sylvia Abergil, who told me to throw away my list. Although it took me a while to actually get rid of it, I can never thank her enough for this wise advice. I will soon tell you why but for now, let me just say that this was the beginning of the end of my "oh, so mental" search.

Obsolete: List of What I Am Looking For in a Man
1. *Must be able to make me laugh.*
2. *We have stimulating conversations.*
3. *He is financially secure.*
4. *He is friendly and loves animals.*
5. *Cannot be addicted to his mother.*
6. *Has a lot of blah blah blah.*
7. *His blah blah blah is his priority.*
8. *Meets his blah blah blah daily.*
9. *He blah blah blahs with everyone.*
10. *Wherever he goes, he blah blah blahs.*

Damn That Intuition, It Just Won't Let Me Go

My frustration with meeting men who did not fit my dream and/or my list reached a screeching crescendo. Even in the stupor that had me chasing my own tail I could hear it loud and clear. I finally threw out my list and took a break from the online dating sites.

It was around mid-May 2010 when I suddenly got the urge to call Gabor. I had no idea why and was very reluctant to follow this impulse. My mind kept saying, "Don't go there. You've tried, and it didn't work," and "You've now been single for 18 years but who's counting? You just don't have what it takes to be in a relationship." But my heart would not leave it alone. In fact, I tried to ignore it for three weeks. Nonetheless, on Friday, June 11, I was bursting at the seams with this nagging feeling. I called my daughter during my lunch break and asked her what I should do.

"Just call him, mom!" she said. So, I hung up the phone and called Gabor. We had a wonderful, long, relaxed conversation, and planned to meet for dinner that night.

The Spark That Ignited My 90 Degree Turn

On the way to our meeting place a remarkable thing happened that changed my life forever. It was actually the most "undoing" thing I had ever done up until that point, and yet it was indeed most fruitful and rewarding on all levels of existence.

As I began to drive, it suddenly dawned on me that maybe, just maybe, the reason my previous attempts to be with Gabor had failed was because I kept judging him. Looking back, I want to holler, "Ya think?"

"If it is my mind that is holding me back from being with him, I better stop it somehow," I said to myself. "Here is a man with whom I have had several deep and illuminating encounters, yet my mind became agitated, disturbed and filled with resistance instead of letting go of its identity and of the image it had of being a highly spiritual and knowledgeable person."

This shocking observation was a cosmic smack in the face. I immediately stopped the car at a nearby parking lot. I sat quietly for 10 minutes or so and began to release all thoughts. I looked for a place of feeling inside me as opposed to thinking. I stayed with this thought-free stillness for as long as I could. Little did I realize that this was the beginning of a 90-degree shift. Not a 180-degree, which is merely the exchange of bad thoughts for their opposites – good thoughts. This was an act, or non-act, rather, of leaving thoughts behind altogether and transcending them entirely. Without knowing what was happening I was getting a glimpse of this type of transformation.

I was now ready to make the most important decision of my entire life, the solid commitment to myself that when I met Gabor I would remain without any thought, critical or otherwise. I was determined to just be, watch, feel and allow things to occur without the slightest mental interference on my part. With this resolution in my heart I left the parking lot and went to meet Gabor.

Well, what transpired that evening was pure magic. I shall never forget it. There was the embrace from my dreams manifesting in all its unmistakable glory. Amazing! Such profound peace. Unquestionable and unparalleled stillness. And all it took was the conscious decision to suspend thoughts, concepts, analysis and the "oh, so spiritual" identity. Did I mention that this was the best decision I have ever made in my life? What I was searching for was finally right in front of me for the past two and a half years and it was only the fucked-up mind that was concealing this fact from me. Go figure!

This is the real secret of manifesting that they don't tell you in *The Secret* or in most law of attraction books and seminar: letting go of your lists of desired outcomes, situations and conditions but even more importantly, not using your mental apparatus for the purpose of co-creating. It interferes every time.

The mind is in duality and therefore, by its very nature, is bi-polar. Most "wants" spring from "lacks." So even if you do manifest a desire, you can be sure that the opposite from which it originated is not far behind. When the pendulum swings back it can hit you like a ton of bricks. Instead of building up your dreams with mental blocks, it is a far superior practice to dissolve them and be open to receive the gifts which have not been erected by the fear-based associative network of your mind.

Performance/Success =
Capacity - Interference

"Together At Last" Is No Longer A Dream

Now that Gabor and I were together, I began to discover more and more the being he is and most of all, his simplicity, sincerity, and unpretentious nature. There is not a phoney bone in him. He plays no games and genuinely loves and respects everyone from a beggar on the street to his closest friends.

After being with Gabor for several years, I noticed that I was not the only one to have misjudged him. He is, by far, the most underestimated person I have ever met in my life. The reason is quite simple. Gabor does not exude the false and exhibitionist type of humility that is common to most spiritual seekers, as well as unawakened teachers. He is just himself with no intent or attempt to impress or impose.

Even when we finally got together he did not show the slightest expectation that I should follow his lead, learn what he knew or even read any particular book. I felt nothing but full and unconditional acceptance, care and love from him.

We found that we had so much in common. At one point he even asked me if I was his twin sister. The many parallels in our lives were astounding. Although we grew up in distant places, in very different environments, and with dissimilar backgrounds, there seemed to be a mutual thread that allowed us now to connect with each other on the same trail.

In our early years we were both possessed by "the quest for freedom." As we moved into adulthood, our ambitious natures took us in different directions; while Gabor was convinced that freedom could be had by acquiring wealth and power, I had total disregard for money and believed that finding God would give me the freedom I was seeking. It was later on in life that we each realized that the real yearning we each had was to discover our true Home and our original Being.

Rebel "Without" A Cause Meets Rebel "With" A Cause

While I was born in a country that was renewing itself, and in an environment of fresh beginnings, accompanied by the enthusiasm of re-building, re-structuring and re-enlivening the land with new blossoms and nature's best vegetation, Gabor was born in the polluted industrial city of Miskolc, Hungary. This was a country that was struggling to recover from the World War II, a land of chaos, violence, emotional upheaval and poverty.

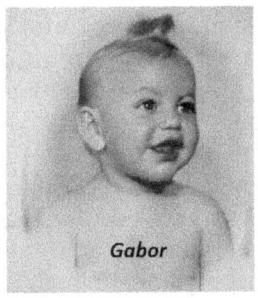

Gabor

Nurit

My parents had to wait for 4 years to have me since the Kibbutz requested all adults to postpone starting their families till the new settlement was completely built. So my folks expected me with great anticipation and excitement. Gabor's parents, on the other hand, after many failed attempts to abort him while still in the womb, finally succumbed to letting him stay, since he was such a cute baby. How is that for a start?

I was thoroughly enjoying my first six happy years of frolicking around, picking rocks, rolling naked in the mud, collecting wild flowers and playing with animals on the beautiful hills of the Galilee with little to none adult supervision.

Meanwhile, in Miskolc, Gabor's first six years never saw a shred of happiness. After the Hungarian revolution against the communist regime, his father was frequently taken away, beaten up and then sent home by the communists who came back into power after the revolution had been subdued.

Whereas I was, at first, a little Pollyanna girl who viewed the world with pink rosy glasses, Gabor was a very sensitive boy who could not get over the fact that there was so much pandemonium, quarrelling, fighting, viciousness and consistent upheaval in this world. He only got some relief during his brief moments in nature. "I would go out and walk among the flowers that were about my height, and I was communicating with them," Gabor recalls. "I just couldn't understand why the rest of the world, humanity, was so ugly."

In spite of these drastic differences – me having all the freedom I could hope for as a child, and Gabor having none – the insatiable lust for freedom was ever-growing in each one of us.

At the age of three or four I was on a field trip to a nearby city with the kibbutz's kindergarten children. Awestruck by the colourful beauty of the flowers at a distance, I broke away from the group and wandered over to be immersed in their captivating fragrance and presence. I had no sense of time so I have no idea how long it took for me to realize that I was completely lost in this big city, without a single familiar face around me. Fortunately a kind man (or was he an angel?) appeared and took me to the central bus station. He then put me on the bus to Sasa where the bus driver, a member of the kibbutz, recognized me and brought me home safe and sound with my huge bouquet of stolen flowers.

In Miskolc, Gabor had a lot less freedom than I did. When he was three or four he dug a hole under the fence in his parents' back yard, just as a dog would, and out he went hitch-hiking on a horse and buggy. This was his first escape. "Ah, the pleasure of freedom that lasted one full day," he says. "I could never stand any kind of bondage."

While I lost my freedom at the age of six when my family moved to Canada, and for the first time I had to live with parents, back in Miskolc, when Gabor turned six, his family unit was crumbling. His parents got divorced and his mother escaped from Hungary during the revolution and ended up immigrating to Canada. So with his mother gone and his father frequently being taken away, Gabor constantly moved around from his father's house to his grandparents' or to friends' homes and back again. He now had a lot of freedom, which he cherished more than anything.

People often ask Gabor how his mother's leaving him at such a young age affected him, assuming it was a very sad and traumatic experience for him. At one point I too asked him that question.

"In retrospect, this was one of the best things that happened to me." he replied. "Since I didn't have to learn all my mother's limitations and idiosyncrasies, I consider it a very positive event in my life. I grew up on my own, so I didn't have too many false beliefs and concept imposed on me."

I found this answer very inspiring. In fact, not too long ago I heard that friends of my parents came to our kibbutz in the early 50s with the intention of becoming members. However, they changed their minds and left after seeing me running around in dirty diapers and calling out for my father by his first name. Viewing my situation through the filters of their family values and reference points, they considered my life to be terrible. In their eyes, I appeared neglected. What they didn't realize was that this was actually a great blessing for me, since I was allowed to start my life with very little limiting conceptual impositions. Besides, I had no idea what they thought I was missing.

While I was about to lose my freedom once again by being drafted into the Israeli army, Gabor was executing his next move towards his freedom, the great escape from Hungary. He had no plan. He had always dreamed of going to North America, irrespective of his mother being there. All of a sudden, out of the blue, the right information appeared. His strategy was to cross the border to Yugoslavia and then proceed to Italy. He couldn't tell his father, since that would have put him in great danger. He only told a couple of very close friends who were sworn to secrecy.

He had very little money and no food. All he knew was that he should head west. Crossing the border in Yugoslavia was a bit easier since it was also a communist country. The journey into Italy, however, was extremely treacherous. With much caution and trepidation he finally arrived in Italy in the middle of a very cold night. He slept in a telephone booth for a few nights and prostitutes brought him sandwiches. Nonetheless, he was very happy since he felt he made it. He could almost taste the impending freedom he had been longing for.

After a few days he found out that if he surrendered to the police he would be ok, and so he did. He was taken to a refugee camp. Here he spent six months while his immigration papers were being processed, and then he finally made it to Canada.

Ambition Turning Points – Rags To Riches To Rags

During the period of my intense spiritual ambition, giving all my time, money and attention to my Guru with the hopes of attaining my final freedom, Gabor was on his own mission of making lots and lots of money which he believed, at that time, would offer him the liberation he was seeking.

He learned English very quickly and put himself through university by working at a gas station at night. Gabor chose to major in electronics engineering because he heard that that is where the future is, not realizing how much he actually hated it. He then got into land development and did very well. He was burning with desire and determination to be successful and was willing to do anything to achieve it. His motto became, "Who do I have to kill, in order to get ahead?" I'm pretty sure he didn't slay anyone. Nonetheless, by the age of 30, Gabor was already a multi-millionaire.

At the exact same year that I left my entire past behind, my Indian Guru, the Siddha Yoga teachings, the ashram, all my friends and the USA, and found myself studying intellectual metaphysics with a new teacher, Gabor went through one of the biggest turning points in his life as well. He lost all his money, left his family and moved out of civilization. The next seven years he spent living in a forest near Seattle, WA, and attending the Ramtha School of Enlightenment. He also studied sacred geometry by taking several "Flower of Life" seminars with Drunvalo Melchizedek himself.

From this point on, his ambition for success gave way to his fervent desire for spirituality and self-knowledge. In our own separate ways, Gabor and I now shared the same priority.

Gabor was very impressed with Drunvalo Melchizedek when he saw him at a symposium in Banff, Alberta, in the mid 90s. Drunvalo showed up to his own lecture in the utmost simplicity and humility. He wore a plain t-shirt, running shoes and jeans. There was nothing fancy about him, nor was there any spiritual hoopla. His inner peace was oozing out of him as he walked slowly toward the podium with his head slightly tilted.

People were lined up to go into the hall. There was a lot of noise and a feeling of disorder around. None of this bothered Drunvalo in the least. He did not impose any rules or instructions, nor did he ask people to turn off their cell phones. As soon as one person noticed him the silence in the room spread like wildfire and he began to speak. Drunvalo's peaceful demeanor meant more to Gabor than the sacred geometry that he studied with this man.

Gabor's path also led him to Ecuador, where he spent three-and-a-half months in a jungle with a shaman and a tribe of Indians. This was not a romantic experience for him nor was there a Pocahontas anywhere in sight. The living conditions there were certainly not the best. When he got up in the morning he was scratching himself like crazy. He felt rather fortunate that they were mainly vegetarian and ate roots and plants as he wouldn't have wanted to eat the creatures that the Indians hunted.

So while I was studying, memorizing and analyzing the words of Dr. Mills in an attempt to gather more and more knowledge, Gabor was trying to do the same by staying with this tribe. However, the knowledge that Gabor was waiting for was not forthcoming. Little did he realize that he had more of it than they did but somehow, they were the ones who had the stillness.

When he looked around in the morning, Gabor saw that all of the tribe members were sitting around smiling with inner peace and doing nothing. He, on the other hand, was filled with restless anticipation and anxiety inside. He only pretended to have inner peace. About 10 days passed by this way and the Shaman felt that Gabor was at the end of his rope so he began to take pity on him. The shaman had a tea, called Ayahuasca, made for Gabor. The Indians normally drink this tea twice a year to "purify" their spirit, but Gabor ended up drinking this tea twice a week for three weeks.

At the beginning of his experience with the Ayahuasca, a lot of fear came up. However, after that, this drink began to teach him not in the form of pictures, but rather with feeling. So about three weeks went by, and at last Gabor was able to relax completely. Now that he was more at ease, the shaman finally allowed him to participate in the "White Eagle" initiation which took place around a fire to the beating of drums and occasional guttural sounds emanating from the Shaman and others.

> *"How was it possible that these so called primitive yet wonderful people did not have to do anything in order to acquire the inner peace that they were exuding, while I had to drink so much Ayahuasca to calm down, in spite of having so much Knowledge?"*
> *– Gabor*

Chapter Five

MY SPIRITUAL PATH CAN FINALLY START. BRING IT ON!

Ok Dude, Show Me What You've Got

It didn't take more than a few days into our flourishing relationship for me to approach Gabor and say, "I appreciate that you are not trying to teach me anything or impress me with what you know, yet I feel that you have something that I don't get. I have no idea what it is but I intuitively sense that you are for real. I have been with several false teachers, including my ex-husband. You just don't have that façade. You are very different in your behaviour, attitude and words. By now I have had enough experience to know if you were a fake, and you are definitely *not*. Don't ask me why, but I totally trust you and, somehow, I recognize that you can teach me what I am missing."

Before I get to Gabor's reply, which changed my life forever, let me alert you to the fact that the events, realizations and internal happenings that followed may not be written in a sequential pattern, since after my initial awakening time became less and less of an influencing factor in my life.

And The Nirvana Oscar Goes To: What? No Spiritual Hoopla?

So here comes Gabor's very long, complicated and exciting initiation speech:

"It's very simple. Look at me, and feel your hand without looking at it. Notice that your mind will stop."

As I was following these complex and intricate instructions (LOL) and felt my hand more intensely, to the exclusion of all else, something shifted inside me. It was a very subtle, indescribable, indefinable and an ineffable inner most sensation of wholeness, wellbeing and peace. Even what I just said here is an inaccurate elucidation of this "non-eventful" occurrence. The mind was at a complete standstill. There were neither knowledge, understanding nor explanation, just a simple feeling of *"now I get it."*

> To get the depth of what you just read,
> please take a look at the following short video clip called
> "Functional Silence" - https://www.youtube.com/
> watch?v=2g4luu31p0I&feature=youtu.be

Fuck The "Yeah But"

Fortunately for me, Gabor was extremely observant and very skilled at catching the mind at its tricks. Just before my highly developed intellect had a chance to make its futile attempt to re-enter and claim its position, that usually starts with a "Yeah, but," Gabor looked at me very intensely and said, "This is IT."

It seemed easier to "get it" than to get that "This is IT," if you get my drift. So, seeing that he did not receive the response he was waiting for, Gabor grabbed my shoulders, shook me a bit, and while raising his voice to a booming sound of conviction, he repeated, "No! This is it! This is The IT!"

The simplicity of his words washed over my now vacant head and being blonde was no longer a factor.

> *Me: What do you mean by "The IT?"*
> *Gabor: This is "The IT" you've been searching for.*
> *There is nothing else. There is nowhere else to go.*
> *There is nothing else you need to find.*
> *Me: Ohhh*

The "This is IT" was, by far, the most important instruction that any teacher had ever given me and many realizations began to flood in. From third dimension complexity I had now shifted into the no dimension simplicity, where the former rules no longer applied, and the previous dos and don'ts were rendered invalid. There was no longer a need for any other explanation, clarification or illumination, in spite of all the books and seminars that are still out there. In fact, within two days, I cancelled a 10-day course that I had already paid for.

I now realize that the seemingly insignificant exercise of feeling my hand and putting my attention inside the body is a perfect demonstration of how the mind can slow down or stop in a moment. It provides a taste or a sampling, if you will, of where this path is leading, i.e. to a "no thought" realm of enlightenment which is the only real place for any magic to transpire. By the same token, it also acts as an "Initial Qualifier" (I.Q.) that tests the seeker's competency, suitability and willingness to accept the utmost simplicity.

If one is simple enough to be capable of feeling something so totally out of the ordinary and to notice the difference, even though his or her mind can no longer function as an adequate evaluator, then there is a good chance they will get the "This is IT," in spite of its unexciting nature. They will most likely get the importance of this and wish to pursue it further.

On the other hand, if one's mind is so thick with complexities that there is no willingness to even try this, and we have seen this a lot, as the mind rushes to bring in all kinds of references from the past, then there is no hope in hell that he or she will get it at that point. If while reading this you feel that it is too simple to be of any value to you, I suggest that you put this book down. You won't get anything out of it unless you have some kind of aptitude and heartfelt desire for *freedom from complexity*. You might want to watch the video clip mentioned above if you haven't seen it yet, or re-watch it if you have.

So I Am Present. So Now What?

So, although stilling my mind by entering my body was and still is the greatest gift I have ever received, I have yet to master it and sustain it, which is the hardest thing in the beginning of awakening. The mind simply won't have any part of it and does its utmost to jump back into the rink and take over.

Nonetheless, my long search of nearly 40 years was over. It was wonderful to realize that I had found the way to accomplishing my life's mission. I am free at last of all spiritual false restrictions, impositions, delusions, future decoys and dangling carrots. Not only that, but I am now spiritually independent. I can now Be What I Am, return to my original self, and be Home instantly. No waiting, no hoping it would rub off from someone else, and no anticipation that the next course will do it. No one can fool me and I know without doubt that it is here and now, it is within always. I know this not by hearsay but from my own experience. There is nothing to be found "out there" and nothing to add or subtract in the future.

Someone finally showed me the "how" and it cost me nothing. It was free and took no time at all. The only price I *did* have to pay was emptying myself of all thoughts, concepts, expectations, pre-requisites, etc. This was indeed a gift. But now what? So I am present, so now what?

This important question was now directed back to me. The awakening was instantaneous, but after such a long search the seeking itself became a way of life, a habit that has been deeply seeded and imbedded in me, and the mind was counting on this addiction for its existence and for its ability to remain in control. It lived on hope for so many years. Hope was my mind's food, panacea and life line. Having no more yearning, spiritual ambitions and future promises was not something it was willing to surrender to without a mighty fight for its prestigious survival.

The mind learns everything we do. It has soon figured out that while I am present in my body it has no place, and as long as I am living in the present moment without entertaining stories and identities from the past, or dreams of a better tomorrow or even the next moment, for that matter, it has no significant purpose in my life. The mind has now recognized that when spontaneity takes precedence and "not knowing" what comes next is no longer a discomfort, it loses its edge. It shakes in its mental boots every time I am able to detect and eliminate an ego-tendency, and does its utmost to find a better hiding place.

And worst of all, when thinking, acquiring new knowledge, describing and analysing seem to lose their appeal and charm, and fancy words no longer dazzle me, the poor old bastard is at the end of its rope. Bottom line, my mind has begun to face its own doom.

The feeling of being squashed and the prospect of being deemed irrelevant has caused it to do its best to get back in control and claim the throne that never belonged to it in the first place. Fortunately, Gabor has been there every step of the way, guiding me out of the persistent mental maze, all the while addressing the mind, not me. This has been helping me to break away from the identity with the mind and become less reactive while stripping away old habitual thought patterns, including the one on devotion which I had been so attached to. Yes indeed, I soon learned that even devotion is a mind-made concept. My original self has now started to claim its rightful place and this has all been happening inside on a heart and soul level.

There is now no longer a need to place anyone else on a pedestal, and the necessity for spiritual information as a means to "getting there" has been dropped. When I read books or watch videos of other teachers, it is merely a way of enjoying their presence, and I can now easily tell who is for real and who is not. I finally get Eckhart Tolle. His words, as well as other genuine teachers such as Mooji, Leonard Jacobson, or Gabor Harsanyi, are now listened to with no reference points from the past and no comparing and analysing thought processes.

As long as I can remain present by being anchored in my body I can truly hear what those teachers are saying. If the mind is doing the listening, the words seem very uninteresting since words, coming from a silent space, do not impress the mind. This is the reason why many people who are lost in their minds claim that Eckhart's books and lectures are boring and they search for speakers who can excite their intellects, as I have done for so long. I now know that it is only the mind that gets bored. Listening with presence is a whole different experience.

Holy Shit. How Did I Miss That?

One of the first insights that popped up almost immediately for me was that I was able to awaken through Gabor since he was awake. By the same token, I was never able to Get It before, because none of my prior teachers were fully present. Furthermore, now that I was able to truly step out of the mind, as opposed to "thinking" I wasn't in it, it became very clear to me that the past teachings I was studying were, in fact, given by a mind to my mind. This was not a pleasant consideration. I felt as though so many years had been wasted and this opened the flood-gates for emotions of being misled and betrayed to come rushing in.

Some people say that any previous teaching is good since it is a preparation for the Real one. Let me assure you that this is a farce. Former misguided teachings are not a warm up nor do they loosen the spiritual pickle jar for the next mentor. The more spiritual knowledge or content that is acquired, the bigger the conceptual ego-based boulders that have to be removed. Trust me on this one. I am still chipping away at some of the rocks that I had allowed Dr. Mills and other teachers to place on my path.

As my mind began to make its attempts to get me back into the third dimensional spiritual drama, one of the first and toughest topics it picked was the many years wasted searching in the wrong places and learning from inadequate teachers. Initially, I wanted to defend and excuse my previous mentors and play the devil's advocate on their behalf.

Following is one of the dialogues I had with Gabor, due to the pain of perceiving the trap I was in with Dr. Mills. Looking back, my questions seemed quite ignorant, but I chose to expose this here for anyone who may have experienced the shock and initial despair of feeling "How the fuck could I have been so wrong for so long." Hey, I got conned twice!

> *Me:* *Did I have to be with a teacher like Dr. Mills because I was not ready to hear the Truth? Should I not be taking responsibility for manifesting someone who misled me?*
> *Gabor:* *Sure, from the mind's perspective, according to the law of attraction, you could say that. However, this is nothing but mental masturbation.*
> *In advanced business schools they teach, "Communication is the*

*response you get." In other words, the responsibility lies with the person teaching. Dr. Mills spoke with his intellect to your intellect. It was a mind to mind attraction. It would have been ok for him to just teach you meditation, but to facilitate awakening a teacher **has** to be awake. This cannot happen through the intellect. Teaching it intellectually in words is like trying to prove the existence of the moon by how many dogs are barking at it.*

Me: *But if he **was** awake, would I have gotten it?*

Gabor: *That question is irrelevant, because you cannot speculate what would have happened in the past. However, knowing that he had your ear, your heart, your full attention and dedication, and that you would have accepted anything from him, I would suspect that you could have woken up if he had been truly awake. You **did** have all the necessary ingredients. Give me a student with that attitude, commitment and characteristics, and I **will** initiate him or her.*

*The teachings you received were given conceptually. Going within as a concept is not the right direction. I get that it is not easy to come to terms with the fact that you have been going the wrong way for so long, but some people need to go through several extremes so that they learn, once and for all, where **IT** isn't. You can never be fooled again.*

I am sure Dr. Mills had moments of presence, or he wouldn't have been able to paint, compose, and be so creative. Many great artists experience this, but the problem with most is that their creation is celebrated instead of the source from which it has sprung. He wasn't able to teach you how to be present, since he didn't master it himself. What was missing was a teaching of simplicity, devoid of reference points, verbal or otherwise.

Me: *Some teachers say that a student may not be ready for simplicity, because of blocks that need to be handled, or stuff that has to be learned before they can be awakened?*

Gabor: *Even if a teacher suspects that a seeker has an impediment of sorts and might be in need of some kind of therapy, if he acknowledges this in any way the student's mind would start to rejoice since now there is a process in which time is involved. The moment the instructor accepts and makes you aware of any kind of pre-requisite for awakening, or an obstacle that needs to be removed, in order to be present, that mentor has stepped over the boundary of intellect versus being.*

The job of the teacher is to be in "Being" for the initiate. No matter how little, if I acknowledge the tiniest obstacle or need in you, that would create a future event and I would have sold you to the devil. My words as a guide are secondary. Any implication that there is a process that is complex would be leading you back to the mind and I would succumb to the ever-changing, ever-conning trickery of the mind.

"Be with me" "Be with me" "Be with me" is the teaching. Being in presence for a while might elicit a process within you which an outside observer would interpret as the removal of a block, or a spiritual cleansing, such as Kundalini awakening. However, to make the said cleansing a pre-requisite to awakening is a crime. It is a poison. As an after effect, it might be a natural consequence. And, by the way, there is no list of after effects.

Any precondition, suggested by the teacher, is nothing but the latter's ego's attempt to put himself on a higher level.

Till this day, I am still finding it hard to write these harsh words about a teacher I once loved so much, that I was completely oblivious to the havoc he created in my spiritual development.

Noticing my resistance, Gabor recently said, "It seems strange to me that an intelligent person like you, who spent 15 years in a 'spiritual concentration camp' with Dr. Mills, a teacher who spoke behind his students' backs, took their money, time and their minds, and imposed a life style on them that he himself wasn't following, after all this time you are still finding it hard to say out right that that king had no clothes. It seems like he continues to have a hold on you."

Perhaps I needed to go through this experience because my personality, as a zealot and a blind follower, had to come to a head, like an abscess that has to get bigger before it can burst and heal. This is what it took to deplete my spiritual drive. And the truth is that I became completely and utterly spiritually exhausted. By the time I met Gabor my head was spinning with a tremendous amount of spiritual knowledge, experience and content.

Funny, I thought the path to enlightenment would make me lighter but instead, I felt more like a beaten up sumo wrestler, desperately trying to pick myself up from the enormous and burdensome weight I was clinging on to as my spiritual drive was finally coming to screeching halt. In order to go inside, any ambition is nothing but a hindrance. Mine had to be diminished and the universe did not care how this would be accomplished.

> *Me: In the past, I put so much effort into my search and had commitment and loyalty to a flaw, literally. Now that I have finally found the truth, I am spiritually exhausted and don't seem to have the same drive, yet I cannot give up. I feel like an employee who spends years perfecting her skills and sucking up to all the right people and when she finally becomes the CEO, she has no more hutzpah to push forward.*
>
> *Gabor: You were building your spiritual achievements with effort, and*

got addicted to this process. Now, the strategy, or the modus operandi, has shifted to flowing with the river effortlessly.

What helped me quite a bit in my early days of awakening was a video I saw of an interview with one of Gabor's past teachers. In the first part of it he confesses that for years he taught and said all the right things, but he was speaking from his intellect without ever having awakened. It was years later, after a calamity in his life, that he became present, and now he can teach from the new dimension. It was so wonderful to hear this humble account. How I wished I could have heard Dr. Mills say the same.

Is You Is, Or Is You Ain't, the Body?

Another important question I had for Gabor had to do with the body. I remember calling him late one evening, since the whole idea of using the body to find God was unlike, or rather contrary, to anything I had ever learned.

Me: *You guided me into this so-called meditation where you asked me to feel my hand, then other parts of my body, and finally to feel the inner energy of the body. As I did this with you, something opened up for me. I felt such peace, presence and stillness. With open eyes, and looking and walking around, I kept feeling the inner body. I was able to be in perfect inner stillness while my legs and eyes were engaged with the world round me.*

For years I was in teachings that looked down upon the body, implying that you can't find divinity in it since you can't put the greater into the lesser. One teacher called the body a "shit factory," while another describe it as "salt, water, chalk, protoplasm and slime, all slung together in this bag of time." I was told that we are not the body and that we should not identify with it. So how is it that feeling your body, which is supposedly inferior, helps one to be present?

Gabor: *The mind's greatest con job is to attract teachers who warn you against identifying with your body. No one really does identify with the body. People identify with their minds and stories, not with their bodies. It is just a hoax to keep you less and less in touch with the body which provides an entry to the universal intelligence inside, which makes it all work so beautifully.*

The notion that we are not the body is totally a faulty spiritual concept. If I needed to somehow explain in words who I am, or who we are, I would use words like, "We are part of God," or "We are everything," or "We live in every blade of grass," etc. I would not use the phrase, "I am not the body." I could say, "I am not **only** the body." That would be more accurate. Not only is "I am not the body" a faulty statement, but, if believed, it would exclude one of the most important components to self-realization, which is what I call "the door."

Why is it that Jesus's famous claim, "The kingdom of God is within," is not emphasized in most churches? The body is of utmost importance because, if used properly, it is a very sensitive door or opening which allows us to find our true Essence.

No one, not even the best doctors, know how the body works. Our minds couldn't possibly run our bodies for two seconds. There are billions of interrelated pieces of information that make the body function as it does. Therefore, if I would be so daring, I might say that God or the Universe is the supreme intelligence that runs my body.

So if I want to get in touch with God, what would be the closest to me that is guaranteed to be part of God? It is my own body. By feeling my hands, or by feeling the inner energy of the body, I am allowed access to the creator of the universe, thereby remembering the original context of life, which can lead to self-realization. This is why feeling your hands is a good lead-in or first step.

"I am the body" and "I am not the body" are both inaccurate statements. However, if I had to pick one, I would say, "I am the body," since it is a door to my Being.

Me: Wow! So for 40 years I've been running around in circles trying to prove my devotion and, subsequently, going about it intellectually in order to find my Self. All the while, what I was searching for was already and always inside of me.

> **Gabor:** Like a dog chasing its tail thinking,
> "Once I catch my tail, I will finally be a dog."

Gabor's Awakening: The Mother Of All Uneventful Events

Me: And how did you find this, how did you awaken?

It wasn't easy for Gabor to narrate the events that led to his awakening, since so many things happened simultaneously. There was no chronological step by step development which could be defined as such, nor was there a sudden burst of, "Aha! I finally got it!" that he could mark on the calendar.

Gabor: *Believe it or not, my greatest teacher was deep suicidal depression. It's amazing how quickly you lose friends at a time like this. If it wasn't for my brother Tom, who always stood by me, I don't know how I would have survived.*

The depression stretched out over a period of 10 years or so, in various intensities, while I was pursuing other spiritual practices and experiences such as living in the forest and attending "Ramtha's School of Enlightenment," endeavouring to make a living by building a condominium in Mexico, hanging out with Indians in the jungle of Ecuador, or simply running around seeking a cure for it.

The depression still lurking around, I was becoming more and more desperate to find ways to rekindle the feelings I had while living in the jungle with the Indians in Ecuador, and the bliss and well-being I experienced while spontaneously swimming like a dolphin for four hours in a pool in Mexico.

This ignited the surfacing of past memories from my martial arts training where I took Karate, Kung Fu and kick boxing, and ended up with a black belt in Hapkido. I began to recall the "secret," or the "super powers," that some masters exhibited, which enabled them to render another almost incapable of twisting their arm.

The secret was going inside one's body, which most people didn't get since it was too simple. As the memories of this technique kept reappearing, I suddenly started to have some success in going into my body. I noticed that whenever I was able to do so I became very calm and my mind would stop.

So now my depression became my main motivator to keep going deeper and deeper inside and anchoring myself in my body. I spent much time sitting by the water and experimenting with grounding my body to the beach. There were moments when, all of a sudden, the sound of the waves became different, and the mind was so still, that there were hardly any remnants of the depression. I would get up and start walking on the beach, and the sand and the water on the feet felt unlike it ever felt before.

If I must name it an "event," this is when it all came together for me. Perhaps the practice of going into the body while walking was the key solution to inner peace. There was an inner knowing with no one to talk to about this. This marked the beginning of the end of the depression. It still reared its ugly head from time to time for a while, but now I finally had the antidote, which happened to also be the solution to life on this planet with its "syphilization" (civilization).

It is interesting to note that prior to my so called "realization" on the beach, I had several preliminary insights and experiences which most likely contributed to it. One was the very important "intellectual" recognition which I had in the jungle with the Indians where I realized that, although I knew so much, I was still missing the most essential thing. Intellectual realizations are usually worthless, but to me, this one was significant, as it prompted me to find the one thing I was lacking.

The other preceding experiences were sensorial and, therefore, more sensational. For example, at the Ramptha School of Enlightenment there were peak moments of feeling extreme exhaustion from dancing blindfolded all night to music and drumming, and several Kundalini upsurges involving hours of simultaneous laughing and crying. And in Ecuador there were the sensations induced by magic mushrooms and Ayahuasca.

Both the intellectual as well as the sensorial realizations always came about as a result of "doing" something. The final and actual realization, on the other hand, appeared on its own. The memories of past techniques arose spontaneously due to feelings of acceptance, acquiescence and surrender which were brought about by the pain of depression, which seemed to have softened me up. This was neither an intellectual nor a sensorial realization. It was neither dramatic, noticeable nor fleeting. It was a rather subtle and uneventful happening beyond the senses and very difficult to describe. It was also permanent.

When I say permanent, I am not talking about it in the same way that most people think. I am not referring here to a continuous state of nirvana in which life's events never bother you. By "permanent realization" I mean a place that exists eternally and can be accessed by going within. It is the lasting and undying natural abode of a human being. From the mind's perspective it is not very exciting, but on a heart level it definitely feels like Home.

About two years after my return to Toronto, Canada, an old friend sent me a set of VHS videos of Eckhart Tolle's lectures that he gave in India. This took me by surprise, since this friend had no money, and these tapes were very expensive, yet he felt compelled to send them to me without being asked. So, although I was not at all interested in any teacher or teachings at that point and felt I had already found what I was looking for, out of respect for my friend, and being curious as to why he had sent such a costly gift, I decided to give the videos a glance.

I randomly picked up one of the tapes, in no particular order, and somehow, the first thing I heard from this dear loving man on the screen was, "Look at me, feel your hand, and your mind will stop."

Within the first few minutes of watching this tape I had my confirmation from Eckhart Tolle, who is now the number one spiritual teacher in the world. So, although it was not essential, I was happy to receive the validation that the simplicity of my realization was correct.

Why Wake Up When You Can Manifest Your Dreams?

And then I asked Gabor about the most popular topic, Law of Attraction and manifesting one's dreams, that had been on every new age corner and site since the "Secret" came out with all its spinoffs. So what's up with that?

Me: *I had been following and practicing a lot of Law of Attraction and deliberate creation techniques, teachings and slogans such as:*
"If you want it you can have it."
"Follow your dreams."
"Let go of resistance."
"Think positive thoughts."
"Tell a new story."
"Behave as if you already have what you are seeking."
I see now that when I am present, none of those are relevant, any more than my dreams and desires are. I would rather wake up from all dreams and let the Universe operate through me.

It was only when I gave up my wishful list and criteria for what my partner should be like that I found you. Looking back, I could never have put you on my list since I didn't even know someone like you existed, but the Universe did, and it guided me to you.

Gabor: *Deliberate creation is great for people who are lost and are convinced they are not lost. The suffering human mind uses its own tools from its messed up past to attempt to bring about a new creation. Good luck with that. By deliberately creating things, you are contributing more to the illusion and there is nothing wrong with it. The only problem is that you are perpetuating your potential for suffering. Certainly, if you are not awake yet, it is better to attempt to create a better illusion than the one you already have.*

We live in an ever expanding Universe that goes through cycles of involution and evolution. In the involution cycle we create and create and create, in order to expand and have contrasts and resolutions, so that the Universe can work its way out of it and back to its Essence, which is the evolution. This is the way it gets to know itself, or realize its Essence. If the

Universe did not create, it would have no reference point from which to know its own existence.

If everything was yellow there would be no recognition of yellow as such, since there would be no other reference point to identify anything as other than yellow. But when other colors are created then we know what yellow is, since it is not green, blue, or any other color, but yellow. By knowing what isn't, we realize what is.

When you attempt to create with the mind, you are subject to its polarized nature. In other words you are dealing with the thing you want and its opposite. You want something because you are experiencing the lack of it. So when you try to create it you are bringing into the equation both the thing and the lack of it. This way you will have to keep creating what you want in order to escape what you don't want. It is much better to clear yourself of all thoughts, to relax into the empty space of presence, and to allow the Universe to bring you what is essential for you.

> **Life gives us an event. We perceive it as a problem.**
> **We worry. Our minds find a temporary solution.**
> **We believe we fixed it.**
> **Now we have a more favorable situation.**
> **As we repeat this, we start trusting the process:**
> **"Worrying + Thinking = Ability to improve our circumstances!"**
> **Alternatively, if we embrace the event without judging it and allow it to transform us, chances are that the situation will be changed as well and in a more permanent way, since now we begin to trust the universe and we create from a new platform.**

You may make suggestions to the Universe, but if you are still and resting in silence as you do so, you are merely whispering to the Universe instead of screaming at it. The more you want something, the more you are telling the Universe that you are dissatisfied with what you already have. This is resistance rather than a state of acceptance, where the Universe can just pour its gifts unto you.

We live in a fear and greed based society. Greed is just another form of fear; "I must have this, so that I can protect myself from not having it." If we are not creating from an awakened place that is beyond these emotions, we *will simply continue to perpetuate and manifest more of the same. In this way we can never hope to improve the taste of our shit sandwich.*

Pollyanna Wouldn't Know The Dark Night Of The Soul If It Bit Her On The Ass

For so many years I idolized and tried to be like Pollyanna, the bubbly one, who only saw the good in everything. I even looked just like Hayley Mills, the actress who played Pollyanna in the movie, when I was around 12 years old. People used to stop me on the street and ask if I were her!

We've all been told time and again, no matter what path we were on, to have only good thoughts and throw out the bad ones. Around Dr. Mills we were reprimanded if our face didn't wear a smile, showing the world what a positive attitude we had, even if we were miserable.

Me: I have heard you use the phrase "positive madness." Most people talk about madness as a negative thing. They would never refer to something positive as madness. Can you explain?

Gabor: Yes, most people consider positive things as good. "It should continue, let's put emphasis on it." It is regarded as something spiritual, as coming from God. And anything negative is coming from the devil or a punishment for doing something bad.

We should consider that anything coming from the mind, positive or negative, is just from the mind. If something positive comes from the mind, it stands to reason that we are going to have the corresponding negativity in duality. So you have got to observe the mind, whether it is positive or negative, with presence, since positivity is equally damaging unless it's observed like the negativity. As a matter a fact, maybe even more so, because we are not aware of this at all and most of us would rather not believe this. Most people just want to accept that positivity is where it's at, so let's be positive.

No, I would say, let's be real. And being real is excluding the mind or better still, using the mind instead of the mind using us. So if I am coming from a clean slate perspective, if I stop my mind and then I use it, then positivity is wonderful. That positive thought will be permanent. It won't flip to the negative since it did not spring from duality. If I am not coming from that silence space, and I am in my mind, then it doesn't matter if it is positive or negative. It is going to be a tough climb up with a shitty end.

It is not about having a balance sheet, whereby the more positivity you put in the more the positivity will win. No, the more positivity we put in

*through the mind the more negativity will come when the pendulum swings
to the other side, as it inevitably will. This is one of those huge misconceptions
out there about spirituality.*

And boy did this spiritual misconception ever come to bite me in the
ass! For years I had been practicing the cultivation of appropriate spiritual
attributes and the suppression of hurt, problems and anything that would be
considered deleterious or unholy. My Indian Guru referred to all negativities
as coming up by way of the Kundalini's attempts to clean up our chakras
from past impressions. They were to be ignored and we were to focus on our
future bliss.

Dr. Mills used to say that undesirable emotions, tendencies and
propensities are simply there, since they are coming to give themselves up.
This is quite accurate. However, rather than dealing with these emotions, we
were to disregard them and put on a happy face. We were also expected to
neither tell others about any of our problems nor listen to them about theirs.
You could be lying on your death bed but god forbid someone should detect
that something is wrong with you. When my husband left, two of my best
friends suddenly decided to have nothing to do with me to ensure that my
painful feelings wouldn't rub off on them and tarnish their "positive spiritual
disposition."

Between teachers offering eloquently stated verbal solutions and
explanations on overcoming what the spiritual mind and world-think
ignorantly determines as "Bad" or "Negative," and my own need to please,
I had become an expert at "transcending" difficulties with my intellect. I
never noticed that in actuality, I was really becoming adept at escaping pain,
suppressing negative emotions and avoiding discomfort. Congratulations to
me. I had officially become a metaphysical roadrunner.

After my awakening, I began to see clearly that I was sitting on a heap
of concealed garbage, a shit load of unattended and ignored injuries that
were starting to rear their ugly heads, in an attempt to be acknowledged,
seen through and redeemed. This created a tremendous and overwhelming
gloomy period for me, or what is called "The dark night of the Soul," which
very few teachers ever talk about, and for which there is only one solution,
going inside and being anchored in presence.

This answer is so simple and subtle that, at times, my resistant intellect
would take over and I'd say, "My pain is so deep, I need something equally
potent and dramatic to get myself out of this. How could "just being" fix it?
Can a feather duster ever clean up a desert?"

Getting Gotten

I am so grateful that Gabor has never been afraid to speak with me about my grief and has always been able to share his own similar experience. For a while now, he's been the only one who truly "gets me." We've had several wonderful conversations about the difference between understanding someone or something and "getting it" or "getting someone."

Gabor: Understanding is based on previous knowledge that you assume is correct. To use the mind properly in the understanding mode, I must be able to NOT think and wait for the information to come forth calmly. The next step is to compare it with existing experience-based knowledge in the mind, and only then I can form an intelligent opinion. This is the correct use of the mind in an understanding mode. You are in control and you use the mind accordingly. This is the intelligent way to use the mind and education.

In "getting it," there may be some understanding components, but this is beyond understanding. "Getting it" is the act of embodying knowledge where there is no thinking and no longer searching in the mind for comparisons and solutions.

For example, someone tells you a painful experience. With understanding, you would begin to find similar information or narratives in your own mind and compare them with the situation you just heard. Most of the time, people don't even wait long enough to hear the other's complete story before they do this, and then they express some words of comfort and perhaps throw in some advice. At best, this would offer temporary relief, but more often than not it really doesn't do anything. It may even invalidate the other person all together.

Someone might tell you that they are having a problem with their son, who can't keep a job, and you go into your memory bank, compare a similar situation that occurred with someone you once knew, and then you might come up with the words, "Why don't you encourage your son to join the army?" This would probably be totally irrelevant to the situation at hand.

People want to be heard and gotten. They don't need advice based on someone else's narrative. "Getting" a person with a problem means to embody their pain. It entails BEING with it, neither in thought, nor in mind, with no comparisons, just pure Being. Now you can DO something with it. At this point, you are in a position that we call a magician, which is actually normal. What we normally call normal is the stupefied version of normal.

Now you can be an alchemist with that person's situation, and you can do the job as a human BEING – you feel it, BE with it. You might say a few short words such as forgiveness, harmony, flow, etc., without any attachment to the concepts of those words. The doing here is being with it, with no rushing and no thinking. This way you neutralize the problem and send it back to the source. This is not a temporary solution. Getting gotten is the best gift you can give someone. You take the time to get them, listen, embody, and BE WITH. Otherwise you can't really help them. You can only poison the situation.

A problem does not come to you to be fixed. It comes to be embodied and neutralized. When the problem is in the body of BEING it is nullified. It is no longer a good or bad event, and you get transformed in the process. You get deeper into being. The situation comes to die, while you get transmuted.

**Our habit of labelling things and events as good or bad
is primarily predicated upon the degree of control
we think we have over them.
The universe does not label anything.
Its selection criteria is usually based
on what is useful or suitable in the moment.**

A Problem Is Not God's Way Of Pissing You Off

Gabor has spent hours with me during my lowest moments of depression, accompanied by endless tears of doubt and self-loathing, as past issues began to well up out of nowhere. He has never judged, nor has he ever attempted to change anything. He has always provided the spaciousness of presence, or a "no-thought" arena, that enabled my soul's pain to be released from years of suppression. Thus, he has taught me, and demonstrated time and again, how to transcend the dimension of mentality that is locked in the vault of positive and negative concepts.

Through his depression Gabor learned to view challenges as opportunities and as a means to deepen into presence. He often quotes St. Francis of Assisi who said, "Hell is the road to heaven."

Just as a fireman is trained to run **into** the fire and not **away** from it, Gabor taught me not to run away from agony or an uncomfortable feeling no matter how painful, but rather to feel it fully, while being present, so it is allowed the attention it seeks, and is offered to the Original Self, the God within.

Now that Gabor showed me how to enter the door of the body and be present with whatever shows up, without labelling it good or bad, or having any other reference point associated with it, I no longer have the need to be frantically searching for quick mental fixes that only cause issues to come back over and over again.

By the same token, I have learned to be open and available to listen and hear about the suffering of others and to be there "in presence" for them, without the fear of being affected by their pain. I have watched Gabor listen to people on the street who have talked his ears off for hours telling him their life story with all their problems, and he becomes an empty vessel of stillness for them, after which they walk away with a smile. I guess that is the secret to his great listening skill.

> *"Firemen are trained to go into the fire, not to run away from it.*
> *The problems you face ARE your seminars.*
> *Life is your teacher." – Gabor*

Time To Get Out Of The Pigpen

One of the main blocks I have been learning to observe and dissolve, and have discussed at great length with Gabor, is the mind's trick of confusing happiness and "aha moments" of intellectual understanding with presence.

Me: For so many years my "feel good" sensation revolved around getting an intellectual high after reading or hearing a spiritual statement that my mind understood. Never did I realize how this feeling was supplanting the need to actually BE the answer. I have now come to see that there is a vast difference between these good feelings and the peace of being present.

Gabor: "Aha" moments are great and very useful in the so called accumulating phase of your life, for example, earning a degree, learning a skill, playing a sport or a musical instrument, etc. You have to have your high school diploma before understanding university, or you have to know how to hold a tennis racket properly before learning how to do a backhand or a forehand.

If you are not doing well in your tennis game, and the coach says, "You are not holding the tennis racket correctly," you get an "aha" moment. If you discover that holding the racket the right way will prevent mistakes in upcoming games, you have your "aha" moment. In other words, you are satisfied knowing the reason behind the instruction.

"Aha" moments mainly happen in the mind. Even if you have a "spiritual aha" moment "about" awakening, it is happening in the mind, and this is one of the mind's biggest con jobs to make you think that you are making progress towards your awakening. It will go to any length to make you believe you are inside.

The mind has the ability to create very sophisticated systems in order to deflect your attention away from the inner orientation. This process can continue forever, without you ever touching or experiencing your essential spiritual reality. The most it can do is provide momentary relief or satisfaction, much like the temporary re-organization of the dirt and garbage in the pigpen.

"Aha" moments are only useful in the building part of your life, when accumulating knowledge is where it's at. However, in the awakening part of your life, where intellectual knowledge, at best, serves as a scaffolding which must be discarded immediately after explanations, "aha" moments become obstacles. When the mind thinks it understands spiritual concepts, it stores these insights away as, "Now I understand, I get the meaning of this." So basically, that prevents you from having the direct experience. This process of the mind is very powerful, addictive and an excellent way to keep you from ever waking up.

There is a skill (sorry to call it a skill!) to awaken you to your original version, and it usually happens through tragedy or a shock, or it could be a learned skill, which should be called an "un-learning" skill. The basis of this "un-learning" skill can be acquired from a book or a tape. However, because of its simplicity, the mind would label it as ridiculous, or even stupid, and it will dismiss it as if it were garbage.

In my experience, however, after this basic "un-learning" skill, you need a qualified teacher, who lives in the present moment himself/herself. The elementary part is easy. The second part is much harder. Your teacher's job is to protect your awakened self from your mind by proxy.

Me: *I noticed that my mind loves realizations. They give it a sense of purpose and importance. It is born to think, analyse, compare, evaluate, etc. Its favorite sensation is the feeling that "it knows." This is its source of confidence. There is nothing scarier for the mind at the beginning of awakening, or anytime for that matter, than the shaky grounds of not knowing. There is no greater sacrifice for the mind than to give up its ability* *to know. That's why I appreciate it when you remind me that I don't need to know something or other. It is not always easy, but there is great freedom in becoming comfortable with not knowing.*

Gabor: *When one starts to awaken to that which the mind cannot fathom, to a "no-thing" that it is incapable of evaluating, quantifying, qualifying, describing or adjudicating, the mind then loses its control. As long as we still share an identity with it, we too feel insecure and out of balance.*

Me: *We tell ourselves that we are doing ok, since we finally found the truth, and yet there remains a part of us that is not still at all. The mind now has a new covert mission to save us from this embarrassing plight of instability and it develops within us a secret craving for realizations and moments of "Aha!" or of "Now I can finally explain this."*

When these emerge, the intellect is thrilled. "Oh boy, once again I can participate. There is a ray of sunshine, of hope. I may regain control someday after all." It thrives on these crescendos, which offer such a rush that is often mistaken for spiritual bliss, illumination or even presence.

Gabor: *IT ISN'T spiritual bliss nor illumination. Anything on a deep level of presence is not sensational. The real Kingdom of God within is not in the realm of excitement, enthusiasm and mental satisfaction. It is subtler than the subtlest. It is tinier than a mustard seed. And yet, it bears the power to move mountains, if one has faith.*

Not the blind faith that every fake teacher and his uncle talk about in their future-promise dissertations. True faith is the rich soil where the mustard seed can grow and become a plant, even though we have no clue how this happens. That fertile ground can only be a thought-free space. It is a field of pure existence in which the mind's complicated and disturbed threads inevitably melt away, just as an object automatically falls due to the unavoidable pull of gravity without any need of "doing." It is the land where "being" is facilitated in order to be re-discovered, and knowledge and words are secondary at best.

Once and for all, we have to leave the mind out of this, no matter how hard it tries to regain its control. Letting it in for even a miniscule evaluation is like asking a goat for the following advice: "Hey goat, what security system would you recommend that I use for storing my cabbage?"

> ***Don't be fooled by the statement***
> ***"There is always light at the end of the tunnel!"***
> *If we aren't BEING the light within the tunnel, the promised light at the end will only be an elusive interlude, before the next tunnel presents itself with its benevolent darkness.*

FINAL SPIEL AND TESTAMENT

Basically, all paths are great and all paths are fake, depending on whether or not you have hit the mother lode – the INNER silence, the supreme intelligence that really has no name, no term, no concept, no thought, nothing known or unknown, no opposite, no likeness, no NOTHING!

It is only from the platform of this NOTHING or "no-thing" that any practice, path, or whatever you wish to call it, has any value or even any validity. Anything else is merely the ego's attempt at enlightenment, relying solely and heavily on the good-will of the mind and intellect, who are ever available and ready to take the credit for what is considered to be the ultimate attainment in spiritual circles – new age and otherwise.

Teachers who address the spiritual path conceptually, who talk about it instead of demonstrating how to go within by example, who themselves have not awakened, are not only useless but also harmful. They are creating more and more spiritual beliefs and concepts that turn into obstacles which block the entry into the inner realm of silence. Noise in not silence. All concepts are mental noise. Like it or not, this is the truth they are hiding from you so that you will become their life-long student and they will enjoy job security.

Have you ever asked, "How is it that cancer research organizations, which we keep donating to for so many years, never seem to produce any cures?"

Ever wonder about all those thousands of seekers who follow gurus for decades and still don't get what takes only a second to get? Hmmmm. Ever question why their minds are so busy explaining spirituality instead of living it?

By the way, the great Ramana Maharshi, who is considered to be the authority on spiritual attainment, said that the degree of freedom from unwanted thoughts is the measure to gauge spiritual progress. Just saying!

For seekers, the danger of accumulating more and more spiritual concepts, teachings, practices and new approaches goes even deeper since, while they are acquiring their knowledge, so are their minds. When the mind is involved in the search, the mind is actually the enemy. It is learning everything that you are and, believe me, when the time comes, it will use all the instructions you've gathered against you. That's why Gabor says, "You have the right to remain silent. Every spiritual concept you have picked up along your way will be used against you by your mind." And I am the living proof of that.

So what kind of teacher is needed? Well, a boxing coach does not have to be a great boxer at all, he just has to know a lot about boxing and how to communicate this expertise to an apprentice. A music teacher needs to be proficient in music, but does not have to perform on stage in order to train a student to become a great concert pianist. However, if you use the same criteria for choosing a spiritual mentor, you are royally fucked. When it comes to awakening into Presence, one who is not awake or present cannot possibly guide another.

All acquired spiritual knowledge, if not experienced and expressed as such, no matter how famous and accomplished the teacher, can only lead you to the cesspool of spiritual pride. It makes for great conversations and the bliss of name dropping, but it will keep you far away from accessing the sweet yet potent emptiness of silence. As you now know, I've been there, done that and bought the T-shirt, only to find great disappointment. I have written this book in the hope of saving you time and money and sparing you years of frustration.

> **You have the right to remain silent.**
> **Anything you say will be held against you by your mind.**

Remember the prayer I wrote on the note that I placed in a crack between the stones of the Wailing Wall? Well, it has certainly been answered. I have found the love I was looking for both inside and as an outer manifestation called Gabor.

Gabor has been guiding me as a reminder and as a coach to go even deeper within, not by engaging in a planned meditation where time is introduced by having a beginning and an end and where there is an expectation and an agenda. But by being present as much as possible, and for longer durations, whether I am sitting still doing nothing, or whether I am active, and no matter what is happening inside or around me.

Along with this guidance, I have also been privileged to witness a being who lives this way on stage as well as behind the scenes. There are no more surprises or hidden spiritual skeletons for me to discover. I have seen Gabor go through difficult financial situations, life threatening illness and other problems that everyday life throws at one, and I have seen him being praised and acknowledged for great skills. He is always the same – unfazed, unshaken, at ease and serene.

Even when he speaks of his difficult past, which doesn't happen too often, with all it trials and tribulations, there is no charge to it. He is not involved in any story, yet he will dive into anyone's story to help them out of it without being affected and without losing his home base.

The next phase cannot be in a book. It has to be customized and done one-on-one. In his private sessions, Gabor guides an initiate into presence and keeps him/her there until Being recognizes Being, and until one can sense the distinct difference between this feeling and formal timed meditation. Gabor spoon feeds his instructions and leaves no stone unturned. He will expose the subtlest way the ego or mind will pull one out of presence, but he does not make the student dependent on him.

> *If you have not turned inside,*
> *your spiritual path has not started yet.*

CLOSING

As this book comes to a close, it is hoped that it has served as a new beginning to some. If you have been inspired by reading these words and feel ready to turn within, then the following poem is dedicated to you and I welcome a present moment in which we can greet each other, being to being.

FOLLOWING YOUR HEART

Following your heart
Feels like the start,
Of a wonderful new exploration.
You want to shout out
About all you find out,
But whose there for your declaration?

Friends drift away,
To family you've gone astray,
Is this really worth the trouble?
The losses and pains
Seem more than the gains
And life feels like a pile of rubble!

But when your heart breaks into pieces
Don't go **"out"** looking for Jesus.
Just know the treasure is never lost.
For when your mind is at its wits end,
And there is nothing left to defend,
What you find is beyond any cost.

ABOUT THE AUTHOR

Nurit Oren, CPCC, is a Canadian Certified Professional Co-Active Coach, a Certified Witz Management/Leadership Trainer and a Certified Art of Transformation Guide. She is also a published author and an award winning playwright. Over the past 20 years Nurit has helped countless individuals from all walks of life make life-changing decisions from the heart by creating a safe space for inner wisdom and courage to guide them in the right direction and free them from being stuck in unwanted situations.

Having dedicated most of her life to the study of yoga, meditation, spirituality and metaphysics, Nurit excels as a communication, behavior and spiritual consultant. Her background also includes public speaking, coaching speakers, and conducting self-development courses and seminars throughout the United States, Canada, the UK and Hungary.

For more information or to contact Nurit go to www.nuritoren.com

ABOUT GABOR HARSANYI

Gabor is a spiritual coach who frees people from thought addiction allowing consciousness to awaken and to become the real guide.

Gabor is a simple immigrant who nearly lost his life escaping from communist Hungary at the age of 18. He arrived in Canada with a single minded and insatiable thirst and hunger for his first love - power & material wealth. At the age of 30 he already had a black belt in Hap-Kido and was a multi-millionaire, but lo and behold, he wasn't the least bit happy.

And so, Gabor turned to his 2nd love - spirituality. He resided with and was initiated by a Shaman in Ecuador, lived in a forest in the U.S. while attending Ramtha's School of Enlightenment, studied with teachers such as Burt Harding and Bob Proctor, and took a gazillion and one new age seminars - all of which served as soul searching pacifiers with an occasional glimmer of "What a great experience. If only I could hang on to it."

Finally, at the age of 40, Gabor found his true Master — suffering. His suffering came in the forms of heartbreak, the loss his entire fortune and suicidal depression. Through the grace of this newfound master, Gabor was now able to surrender to his 3rd and ultimate love — Presence, the silence of nothing, where the capitulated mind takes a back seat and becomes the servant, and the Original Being is once again seated on the throne!

For more information go to www.gaborharsanyi.com